SIR ARCHIBALD MURRAY'S DESPATCHES

SIR ARCHIBALD MURRAY'S DESPATCHES

(June 1916—June 1917)

WITH SPECIALLY PREPARED
MAPS, AND PORTRAITS

The Naval & Military Press Ltd

Published by

The Naval & Military Press Ltd
Unit 5 Riverside, Brambleside
Bellbrook Industrial Estate
Uckfield, East Sussex
TN22 1QQ England

Tel: +44 (0)1825 749494

www.naval-military-press.com
www.nmarchive.com

In reprinting in facsimile from the original, any imperfections are inevitably reproduced and the quality may fall short of modern type and cartographic standards.

FOREWORD

THE following four Despatches have until now never been published in their full original text. This is especially true of the fourth of this series, dated 28th June, 1917. This Despatch General Sir Archibald Murray is now permitted to publish on the condition that the following letter is published at the same time.

[COPY]

WAR OFFICE,
LONDON, S.W.
4th March, 1920.

121/Mediterranean/5177 (S.D. 5).

SIR,

With reference to previous correspondence on the question of the publication of your despatch of the 28th June, 1917, I am commanded by the Army Council to point out that the various changes of policy on which stress is laid in the first part of the despatch were based not merely on local considerations connected with the campaign east of the Suez Canal and adjacent theatres of war, but on a general review of the course of the war as a whole, including such considerations as the development of the German submarine campaign, the failure of General Nivelle's offensive and the extension of the British line on the Western Front, Allied policy in the Balkans, and the course of events in Russia.

I am to add that, unless this fact is appreciated by the reader, the recital of various changes in policy without relation to events taking place in other parts of the world is calculated to create a somewhat misleading impression.

In authorising the publication of the despatch referred to above the Council must ask, therefore, that this letter be published at the same time.

    I am,
      Sir,
        Your obedient Servant,
         (Signed) H. J. CREEDY.

General Sir A. J. MURRAY,
  G.C.M.G., K.C.B., C.V.O., D.S.O.,
    Went House,
      West Malling, Kent.

EXTRACTS FROM THE DESPATCH
OF
FIELD MARSHAL SIR EDMUND ALLENBY,
G.C.B., G.C.M.G.,
*Commander-in-Chief Egyptian Expeditionary Force,
dated 28th June, 1919*

"By the summer of 1917, when I assumed command of the Egyptian Expeditionary Force, Lieut.-General Sir A. Murray's brilliant campaign in Sinai had removed the danger to Egypt, and had forced the enemy back across his own frontiers."

*   *   *   *   *   *

"I desire to express my indebtedness to my predecessor, Lieut.-General Sir A. J. Murray, who, by his bridging of the desert between Egypt and Palestine, laid the foundations for the subsequent advances of the Egyptian Expeditionary Force. I reaped the fruits of his foresight and strategical imagination, which brought the waters of the Nile to the borders of Palestine, planned the skilful military operations by which the Turks were driven from strong positions in the desert over the frontier of Egypt, and carried a standard gauge railway to the gates of Gaza. The organisation he created, both in Sinai and in Egypt, stood all tests and formed the corner-stone of my successes."

CONTENTS

	PAGE
FIRST DESPATCH.—1st June, 1916	1
SECOND DESPATCH.—1st October, 1916	43
COVERING LETTER SENT WITH SECOND DESPATCH.—11th October, 1916	83
THIRD DESPATCH.—1st March, 1917	87
FOURTH DESPATCH.—28th June, 1917	127
APPENDICES	179
INDEX	221

LIST OF ILLUSTRATIONS

GENERAL SIR ARCHIBALD MURRAY		*Frontispiece*
LIEUT.-GENERAL THE HON. H. A. LAWRENCE	*facing page*	45
SANDHILLS SOUTH OF ROMANI	,,	62
LIEUT.-GENERAL SIR H. G. CHAUVEL	,,	89
MAJOR-GENERAL CHAUVEL AND STAFF OF THE ANZAC MOUNTED DIVISION	,,	101
LIEUT.-GENERAL SIR P. W. CHETWODE, BART.	,,	129

SKETCH MAPS

BATTLE OF ROMANI—SKETCH MAP SHOWING POSITIONS OF BRITISH TROOPS AT 6 A.M., 4TH AUGUST, 1916	*facing page*	64
BATTLE OF ROMANI—SKETCH MAP SHOWING POSITIONS OF BRITISH TROOPS AT DUSK, 4TH AUGUST, 1916	,,	67
MAP OF SIWA OASIS	,,	118

FIRST DESPATCH
1st June, 1916

SIR ARCHIBALD MURRAY'S DESPATCHES

FIRST DESPATCH

From—
    THE COMMANDER-IN-CHIEF,
        Egyptian Expeditionary Force.

To—
    THE SECRETARY OF STATE FOR WAR,
        War Office, London, S.W.

General Headquarters,
Egyptian Expeditionary Force,
1st June, 1916.

SIR,

I have the honour to submit a report on the operations of the Force under my command from the date on which I assumed command to the 31st May, 1916.

1. On 9th January, 1916, I arrived in Cairo, and, on the following day, took over the command of the Mediterranean Expeditionary Force from General Sir C. C. Monro, G.C.M.G., K.C.B., who had himself arrived from Mudros but a few days before. At that date the Mediterranean Expeditionary Force was in a state of transition as regards its larger component, the Dardanelles Army. On the night of the 8th/9th January this Army had completed its successful evacuation of Cape Helles; its units were still concentrated at Mudros and Imbros awaiting transport to Egypt, where all the Force, excluding the Salonica Army, had been ordered to concentrate. Meanwhile a portion of the Force, which had been set free by the earlier evacuation of

the Suvla Bay and Anzac positions, had already arrived in Egypt, where it had come under the command of General Sir John Maxwell, K.C.B., K.C.M.G. The concentration of the Australian and New Zealand Army Corps, for instance, was practically complete, and the 53rd Division was occupied in operations on the Western Frontier of Egypt. General Headquarters of the Mediterranean Expeditionary Force were temporarily established in Cairo.

The instructions which I had received from the Secretary of State for War placed under my command all organised formations then in Egypt, or on their way to Egypt, with the exception of such troops as might be considered necessary for the defence of Egypt and the Nile Valley against attack from the west, or for maintaining order in the Nile Valley and the Nile Delta. The function assigned to me was that of protecting Egypt against attack from the east, and the westward limit of my command was roughly fixed by a line running north and south approximately five miles west of the Suez Canal. The British force at Salonica was also placed under my general supervision. At the same time I was given the important responsibility of maintaining a general strategical reserve of troops for the whole Empire, to be used in whatsoever theatre of war the call should be most urgent.

2. During the period under review, in addition to the extensive military preparations required for the defence of the eastern front, the amount of purely administrative work thrown on all sections of my Staff has been extremely heavy. The exigencies of the Gallipoli campaign had placed the Force under my command in a state of serious disorganisation. Some

units were in Egypt, others on the sea, others in Ægean ports. It was not until the end of February that the last units of the Dardanelles Army reached Egypt. Every day for over six weeks ship-loads of troops, guns, animals and transport were arriving at Alexandria and Port Said. The components of this mass had to be disentangled and forwarded to their proper destinations: old units had to be reorganised, new units to be created, brigades, divisions, army corps to be reformed. The British troops from Gallipoli were incomplete in personnel and material. It was urgently necessary to bring them up to strength, re-equip them, and provide them with train and mechanical transport on a modified scale. The Australasian troops also needed re-equipment, and, in their case, there was the additional problem of dealing with a mass of unabsorbed reinforcements. Further training of officers and men was an urgent necessity. Moreover, the embarkation of troops for service elsewhere began in February and continued without intermission till the end of April. To this work must be added not only the maintenance of my Force, both in Egypt and Salonica, with animals, supplies, ordnance stores, works material, and medical and veterinary stores, but also the provision and despatch of ordnance stores, works material, and supplies specially demanded for Basrah and East Africa.

The bulk of the work of disembarkation and embarkation, including the very heavy work of railway transport, fell upon the staffs of my Deputy Quartermaster-General and Inspector-General of Communications,[1] to whom great credit is due. Between 1st

[1] Up to March 19th the Inspector-General of Communications was also General Officer Commanding Levant Base.

January and 31st May, exclusive of sick and wounded, 10,057 officers, 256,623 other ranks, and 49,969 animals were disembarked in Egypt. The numbers embarked, exclusive of sick and wounded, were 8,507 officers, 202,249 other ranks, and 31,530 animals. The total numbers carried on the Egyptian State Railways during the same period were 67,756 officers, 1,029,499 other ranks, 156,393 animals, 560,300 tons of stores, and 15,518 tons of ammunition. I append a tabular return (see Appendix A) of the complete units embarked from Egypt for service elsewhere. The total includes six complete divisions at full strength, and, in addition, three infantry brigades and nine batteries of heavy artillery, besides signal, engineer and medical units. All six of these divisions were re-equipped or completed with equipment: moreover, transport for two further divisions had to be collected on a special scale; two newly-formed divisions were completely equipped; three further divisions and three dismounted brigades were re-equipped for service in Egypt; five divisions at Salonica were completed with additional pack saddlery to the amount of 20,000 sets, and supplied with very large reserves of ammunition and ordnance stores; a newly-formed Camel Transport Corps and the Imperial Camel Corps were also equipped and provided with animals. This work, together with the task of supplying and maintaining the troops operating on the eastern, and subsequently also on the western, front, was efficiently carried out by the Ordnance, Supply and Transport, Remount, and Works Departments.

As regards the formation of new units, the most important work was that of absorbing the surplus Australasian reinforcements. The New Zealand Division was remodelled so as to consist entirely of New Zealanders, and the constitution of the Australian Provisional Formations under Major-General Sir H. V. Cox, K.C.M.G., C.B., C.S.I., laid the ground-work of two entirely new Australian Divisions, the 4th and 5th, which were actually embodied on 6th March. Steps were also taken to bring the organisation of all the Australasian troops into uniformity as regarded their artillery and other divisional troops. The new Australian divisions took their places in the front line when the 1st Australian and New Zealand Corps went to France, whither they are themselves now about to be despatched. The Australian and New Zealand Mounted Division has been reconstituted, and has proved most valuable both on the eastern and western fronts. In addition, four brigades of dismounted yeomanry have been organised on definite and uniform lines; brigade machine-gun companies have been formed for practically all the divisions in the Force (including those sent elsewhere and at Salonica); Stokes gun batteries for sixteen brigades have been reorganised; the Imperial Camel Corps—a fighting unit—of six companies has been raised and trained for work in the desert, and four more companies are now being trained; the Indian Camel Corps in Egypt have been combined into a Camel Transport Corps, which has been raised from local resources to a strength of 18,000. As regards instruction, a training centre for Australasian reinforcements was started at Tel el Kebir and continued until it was decided that the Australasian training depôts should be transferred to England. Further, a machine-gun school was formed at Ismailia which, after producing excellent results, was merged in the Imperial School of Instruction at Zeitoun (suburb of Cairo). The latter institution, which came under my control after 19th March, has since been increased in size so as to train officers in all branches of warfare. Under its commandant, Lieut.-Colonel the Hon. E. M. Colston, M.V.O., its work has been most valuable. Besides the ordinary courses for officers and non-commissioned officers, it holds machine-gun, Lewis gun, signal and telephone, artillery, Stokes gun, and grenadier classes. Between 7th January and 31st May, 1,166 officers and 5,512 other ranks attended and passed in the various classes. A machine-gun school was also started at Salonica.

Excellent work has been done by the signal service during this period. In the first place, it has efficiently carried out the work of refitting the signal units from the Peninsula, reorganising them to suit the conditions peculiar to Egypt, and training locally officers and men to fill the gaps and meet the increased demand for signallers and telegraphists. Ninety-four officers and 1,305 other ranks have been trained in these duties at Zeitoun and Alexandria this year. Secondly, it has had to provide intercommunication for troops engaged upon over 1,000 miles of front, which has involved the development of an unusually extensive network of military telegraphs. All the resource and ingenuity of the service has been taxed to cope with the conditions peculiar to this field of operations—abnormal distances, unusual means of transport, desert, sand storms and mirage. Lastly, it has substituted a military telegraph and telephone service for the civil system which, until this year, has been the only available means of communication throughout Egypt and was worked mainly by native personnel.

I would also specially mention the survey work

that has been carried out since the arrival of the Mediterranean Expeditionary Force in Egypt. In addition to the standardisation, printing and issue of tactical maps of Sinai to the whole of the Army on the eastern front, a new survey on a large scale of the Canal zone and certain areas east of our lines and advanced posts has been continuously carried on by the Topographical Section of the Intelligence Branch working in close co-operation with the Royal Flying Corps. This survey, which has now been in process for nearly six months, is now approaching Katia. I believe that the map based on this survey is the first map entirely constructed on this principle. The work was initiated by Mr. E. M. Dowson, Director-General, Survey of Egypt, who placed his resources at the disposal of the Mediterranean Expeditionary Force. The actual direction of the work has been in the hands of the Intelligence Branch of my General Staff, and is based on experience, gained in Gallipoli, of the production of trench maps from aeroplane photographs, controlled by ordinary field survey methods. Co-operation in this survey has been part of the routine of the Royal Flying Corps. The main object of the new map thus being produced is to facilitate the co-operation of aircraft and artillery, though it has already proved extremely useful in siting trenches and locating roads, railways and pipe-lines. The system upon which this survey proceeds was devised to obviate the extreme difficulty of surveying large tracts of desert by ordinary methods. Certain areas, from 8,000 to 12,000 yards eastward of our front line, that were likely to include enemy gun positions, were selected and photographed from the air. The photographs were then reduced and fitted by a complicated process to their correct positions on the map. The result has been the attainment of the highest topographical accuracy in the survey of almost featureless desert, which enables observers to " spot " with the greatest precision outside the areas surveyed by ordinary methods.

These labours, most of which demanded the utmost despatch in their completion, were carried out concurrently with the conduct of more strictly military operations, to my report on which I will now proceed.

3. When I arrived in Egypt the intentions of the enemy as regards an attack on the Suez Canal were by no means certain. Though his new means of communication in southern Syria and Sinai, commenced with this end in view, were still in a backward state, he undoubtedly had at his disposal the troops, amounting to 250,000 men or more, necessary for such an attack. The adequate defence of the Canal was therefore a matter of serious importance. The outline of a scheme of defence had already been prepared; certain works were being constructed, railways and pipe-lines and roads commenced, and troops were being concentrated in the three sections of the Canal Defences, which were based on Suez, Ismailia and Port Said respectively. The object aimed at was to construct a front line of defence, suitable for withstanding an attack with heavy artillery, some seven or eight miles east of the Canal. A second, and inner, line was also to be constructed on the east bank, besides certain permanent, fortified bridge-heads. At the same time, the defence of the Canal was to be, so far as possible, offensive, and mobile columns were to be prepared for this purpose in addition to the garrisons for the defensive line. This scheme in outline I took over from the General Commanding in Egypt, under whom it had been operating

for a short time, and, since on January 11th the sole direction of military operations at Salonica was given to General Sarrail, while the responsibility for safeguarding the islands of Lemnos, Tenedos and Imbros was taken over by the Admiralty, I was able to give my undivided attention to the operations in defence of the Canal. I decided to establish my General Headquarters at Ismailia. No. 1 Section, with Headquarters at Suez, was allotted to the 9th Army Corps under Lieut.-General the Hon. Sir Julian Byng, K.C.M.G., C.B., M.V.O.; No. 2 Section, with Headquarters at Ismailia, to the Australian and New Zealand Army Corps under Lieut.-General Sir A. J. Godley, K.C.M.G., C.B., and No. 3 Section, with Headquarters at Port Said, to the 15th Army Corps under Lieut.-General H. S. Horne, C.B. These officers were ordered to take over their commands immediately. The composition of the Force at this time is shown in Appendix B, attached. A satisfactory agreement was arrived at between Sir John Maxwell and myself regarding the delimitations of our respective spheres of command and the troops to be allotted to him. The 53rd and 54th Divisions, two mounted brigades and a Territorial infantry brigade were permanently transferred to his command, and certain other units placed temporarily at his disposal. On 22nd January General Headquarters opened at Ismailia.

My chief concern was now the defence of the Canal. The work on the stationary defences was backward. Difficulties of water supply on the east bank were increased by shortage of piping; labour troubles had delayed the progress of roads and railways. Guns had still to be emplaced, and no part of the front defence line was actually occupied by troops. Nevertheless, as there were no signs of an imminent advance on the part of the enemy, the question of the stationary defences caused me no serious anxiety, though everything possible was done to hasten on their completion. The organisation of the offensive defence, which time has proved to be paramount, was, however, a pressing matter hitherto untouched. Practically nothing had been done towards the organisation of mobile forces. The collection of a large number of riding and transport camels had to be undertaken at once and a plan of campaign to be devised. Moreover, time was short, for it was plain that any offensive on a large scale by the enemy must be commenced before the middle of March. For the Force under my command the only possible line of advance was along the northern line from Kantara towards Katia and El Arish, and the task was at once taken up of examining the possibilities of an offensive on this line and solving the problem of maintaining a considerable force at Katia during the summer months. The result of these investigations is to be seen in my memorandum of 15th February, addressed to the Chief of the Imperial General Staff, in which I stated that the first step towards securing the true base for the defence of Egypt was an advance to a suitable position east of Katia and the construction of a railway to that place. Preparations for this preliminary movement were being actively pushed on. The construction of the railway began immediately, and it was anticipated that sufficient camels would be available to equip a force of one division and one mounted brigade with camel transport very shortly. Such a force would, I then considered, be sufficient to clear and occupy the Katia district and to hold the eastern end of it.

Meanwhile, certain changes had already taken

FIRST DESPATCH

place in the Force, and others had been foreshadowed. The 13th Division had been sent to Mesopotamia, and the 11th Division transferred from the 9th Corps in the No. 1 Section to the 15th Corps in the No. 3 Section of the defences. The 8th Army Corps ceased to exist, and its commander, Lieut.-General Sir Francis Davies, K.C.B., K.C.M.G., took over command of the 9th Corps on General Byng's departure to England.

Up till the middle of February aeroplane reconnaissance was the only active military operation possible, owing to the need for reorganising the units of the Force and for pushing on the work of laying roads, pipe-lines and railways to enable an adequate force to be maintained on, and beyond, the front lines. The magnitude of the latter task may be judged from the fact that, during the period covered by this despatch, 114 miles of road, 154 miles of pipe-lines, and 252 miles of railway [1] were laid. The work of the Royal Flying Corps, most actively and gallantly pursued, enabled me to keep the enemy's posts at Bir el Hassana, Nekhl and El Arish under close observation, and neither their reports nor those of the equally gallant and efficient Naval Air Service, which observed by seaplane the garrisons of southern Syria, showed any concentration of enemy troops for a big attack on the Canal. On 16th February the Russian Army entered Erzerum, inflicting a heavy defeat on the Turkish Army opposed to it. It seemed likely then that all the enemy's schemes for attacking the Canal in force must for the present fall to the ground, and such has proved to be the case. The garrisons in Syria were gradually reduced, until it was estimated that not more than

---

[1] 72 miles of 2′ 6″ gauge, 10 miles of metre gauge, 80 miles of 4′ 8½″ gauge, and 90 miles of Decauville.

60,000 men were available for an attack on Egypt.[1] During the latter half of February the work of reconnaissance beyond the front line began in earnest, especially in the northern section, where the 15th Corps patrolled as far as Bir el Nuss and Hod um Ugba, establishing the fact that the country was all clear and practically deserted. At this period, too, a reconnaissance was undertaken from Tor (see Map 2). This post, and that of Ras Abu Zeneima (see Map 2), both on the Sinaitic coast south of Suez, were then garrisoned by a battalion of the Egyptian Army—subsequently by the 14th Sikhs—and had, by arrangement with General Maxwell, come under my direction. The reconnaissance from Tor was undertaken against a concentration of a small body of the enemy at Wadi Ginneh, some miles distant from the coast. This minor operation was in every way successful, though the enemy had fled before their camp was reached, leaving behind their baggage, which was destroyed. The troops then returned without further incident.

4. From March onwards, the rapid embarkation of troops for France depleted my forces considerably.[2] During this month the military operations on the eastern front, if not momentous, were satisfactory. On 6th March a very gallant and successful attack on Bir el Hassana was made by the Royal Flying Corps, which resulted in the destruction of the pumping station. Bomb attacks were made on Nekhl and other places in Sinai, and on 24th March, Bir el Hassana was again attacked in force with bombs. In the northern sector, the preliminary steps were being taken for the advance to Katia. Week by week permanent posts were pushed

---

[1] See telegram from War Office 16342 cipher, dated 11.5.16.
[2] See Appendix C giving the composition of the Force after the departure of six divisions.

FIRST DESPATCH

further ahead, special reconnaissances were made with a view to testing the water supply, and the broad gauge railway from Kantara to Katia was being carried forward as fast as possible. During this month, also, I gave instructions to all commanders of sections of the Canal Defences which considerably modified the original scheme of defence, as I had taken it over. Starting from the principle that, owing to evaporation of the rain pools, it was now impossible for the enemy to bring up and deploy a larger force than 50,000 men for a sustained attack against the defences, I laid it down that the front line of defence east of the Canal should be looked upon and occupied as an outpost line, the smallest force appropriate to the circumstances being allotted to it, and that all dispositions should be based on the necessity for providing behind it the forces necessary for undertaking a *mobile* defence. Mobile columns were organised in each of the three sections. All were to be provided with camel transport and with camel convoys that would admit of a radius of action of one day's march from the Canal in the case of No. 3 Section, and two days' march in the case of the other two sections. I directed, moreover, that in each section any troops left over after the allotment of units to the outpost lines and the mobile column, should be made sufficiently mobile to operate rapidly at a distance east of the Canal not exceeding half a day's march from road and rail-heads.

5. On 11th March I received instructions from the late Secretary of State for War that the command of the troops in Egypt was to be reorganised and that I was appointed General Officer Commanding-in-Chief all the Imperial Forces in this country, which added to my original command the command held by General

Sir John Maxwell. The preliminary details for carrying this change into operation were fixed at a conference with General Maxwell held on 13th March, and on 19th March I formally took over the whole command in Egypt, thus ending a system of dual control which had of necessity been unsatisfactory, especially from the point of view of economy. By this change I not only became responsible for the administration of martial law in Egypt and the maintenance of order throughout the Nile Valley and Delta, but I also succeeded to the direction of the operations against the Senoussi on the western frontier, which had very appropriately been brought to a triumphant period by General Maxwell by his victories which led to the occupation of Sollum on 14th March, the capture of Gaafer, the dispersal, with the loss of all his guns, of Nuri's force, and the recapture from the enemy of 90 British prisoners taken by hostile submarines. The 53rd and 54th Divisions, the North Midland Mounted Brigade, and other units, including garrison battalions, were added to my Force, besides the Imperial School of Instruction at Zeitoun. The unification of the command in Egypt made large economies in staff possible, and these were carried out at once. The Levant Base also ceased to exist, General Sir Edward Altham, K.C.B., remaining as Inspector-General of Communications. The work of reorganising the forces and staffs for the Delta and Western Frontier Force was pushed on as fast as possible. I decided to keep General Headquarters at Ismailia, and to establish at Cairo a General Officer Commanding the Delta District, who would also act as Commander of Lines of Communication Defences. For operations on the west I formed a Western Frontier Force, divided into two sections, a north-western and a south-western, divided by a line drawn east and west through Darut es Sharif. These staffs and forces were definitely established and at work by 1st April. The whole force under my command now took the name of Egyptian Expeditionary Force. Towards the end of March, at the request of the Sirdar, I undertook the responsibility for the defence of the reach of the Nile between Assuan and Wadi Halfa. Captain F. H. Mitchell, R.N., D.S.O., was sent for this purpose to make all arrangements for an armed naval patrol of this reach.

On 18th March, Captain H.R.H. the Prince of Wales took up his duties as Staff Captain on my Staff, remaining till his departure from Egypt on 1st May.

6. As soon as the conduct of operations on the western frontier devolved upon me, I took steps, in consultation with the various officers who were then best acquainted with the situation, to estimate the size of the hostile forces with which I should have to deal, and to determine the policy along this front of over 800 miles by which the Nile Valley could best be protected. It appeared from the information placed at my disposal that the Senoussi forces, spread over the whole western desert, did not exceed 3,000, and it was certain that the enemy's moral had been severely shaken by Sir John Maxwell's recent successful operations. The chief dangers, therefore, against which I had to guard, were enemy raids upon the Nile Valley, the stirring up of native tribes that were inclined to be well-disposed towards the Senoussi, and the creation of unrest in the Nile Valley and Delta among disaffected or nervous elements of the population. The chief end to be held in view was to prevent any local success on the part of the Senoussi.

B

Had it been possible, the best way of attaining this end would have been the occupation of the Siwa Oasis, which is the focus of all the routes between the Nile Valley north of Assuan and the west. With the Siwa Oasis in our hands, the retirement of enemy forces east of Siwa would have been practically certain, thus eliminating any menace against the Nile Valley and Delta. However, I was advised that it would be impossible to undertake this operation unless it could be successfully carried through within three weeks from the beginning of April. For an operation requiring most careful preparation and organisation, this time was all too short, and I reluctantly came to the conclusion that it must be deferred for the present, though I kept under consideration the question of extending the coast railway from Dhabba to Mersa Matruh, and from there eventually to Siwa. So far as the extreme north-west was concerned, the state of affairs was such as to relieve me of all anxiety. Mersa Matruh and Sollum had been reoccupied, and, as these are the only Egyptian harbours west of Alexandria, their occupation, together with the patrol of the coast undertaken by the Navy, was likely to prevent the enemy from receiving arms, ammunition, or other assistance from hostile submarines within the area under British control. As regards the security of the Nile Valley and Delta, at the moment when I took over command, this was only provided for by the occupation of Wadi Natron with patrols 45 miles out to Hammame and Moghara, the occupation of the Fayum in considerable force, and the posting of small detachments of troops along the Nile as far south as Assuan. The question to be determined was whether Moghara and the westerly oases, Baharia, Farafra, Dakhla and Kharga, through

FIRST DESPATCH

one or more of which any enemy raids would have to pass, should be denied to the enemy by occupation on our part. The conclusion to which I came was that the western defence of Egypt could be fully secured by the occupation of Moghara, the Baharia Oasis and the Kharga Oasis, and that any danger to the Nile Valley between Minya and Girga could be met by subsequently clearing the Dakhla Oasis of enemy troops and maintaining a small force about Assiut ready to move up or down the railway as might be required. I gave instructions accordingly to the General Officer Commanding the Western Frontier Force to make his dispositions for occupying, in the order named, the Kharga Oasis, Moghara, and the Baharia Oasis.

On 15th April the Kharga Oasis, which had previously been reported by aerial reconnaissance and resident agents to be clear of the enemy, was occupied without incident. The movement of troops was effected by the existing light railway, and by the 18th April a force numbering 1,660 of all ranks was concentrated in the Oasis. This force, commanded by Lieut.-Colonel A. McNeill, 1/2nd Lovat's Scouts, consisted of one squadron of Egyptian Army Cavalry, a company of the Camel Transport Corps, three regiments of the 2nd Dismounted Brigade, a section of the Hong Kong and Singapore Mountain Battery, a detachment of the Royal Flying Corps, and a section of the Cheshire Field Company, R.E.

On the 27th April the small oasis of Moghara was occupied by a force consisting of the 2nd Company Imperial Camel Corps and the Denbighshire Yeomanry (dismounted) under the command of Lieut.-Colonel A. H. O. Lloyd, M.V.O., commanding Shropshire Yeomanry, based at El Amaid station on the Mariut railway. A strongly entrenched post has been constructed. The occupation of this post has materially assisted in preventing the passage of foodstuffs from the Nile Valley to the west, and denies the water to any enemy force attempting to move in the contrary direction.

During April frequent raids and reconnaissances, chiefly with a view to capturing concealed depôts of ammunition, were undertaken on the western front: in these enterprises our armoured and light motor cars have been of inestimable value. On 7th April a detachment of four armoured cars, accompanied by the machine-gun section of the 2/7th Middlesex Regiment, conducted a raid from Sollum upon an ammunition depôt at Moraisa, 18 miles north-west of Sollum. After a very slight resistance from the guard of 30 Muhafzia, 21 boxes of 8.9 centimetre Mantelli gun ammunition and 120,000 rounds of small arms ammunition were taken and destroyed. On 11th April a motor-car reconnaissance found and removed 11 rifles and 7,000 rounds of small arms ammunition some 20 miles west of Sollum. On 23rd April an armoured car reconnaissance from Sollum discovered and brought in 140,000 rounds of small arms ammunition from a concealed depôt. On the 30th April a further 20,000 rounds were discovered and brought in to Sollum. During this month, also, four prisoners, including a Turkish officer, were captured 60 miles west of Minya, and two small camel convoys were captured near El Amaid. The light-car patrols were responsible for all these captures.

7. During the month of April, reconnaissance was active all along the eastern front, with the result that by the middle of the month all water supplies of any

FIRST DESPATCH

importance within 30 miles of the Canal were patrolled by our troops, and mobile columns were ready to go out and deal with enemy parties approaching them, or, in the event of serious threat, to demolish the rock cisterns. In No. 1 Section, on 20th April, a patrol from Bir Mabeiuk came in contact with an enemy patrol, 50 strong, on the sand-hills near the mouth of the Wadi um Hamatha, some 18 miles W.S.W. of Suez. A squadron and 50 rifles endeavoured to cut the enemy off, but he at once retired and scattered among the hills. Our casualties were two men killed. On 23rd April and the following days, four columns, each composed of mounted troops and infantry, carried out reconnaissances of the approaches from the west to Ain Sudr and Sudr el Heitan. The columns returned to their respective posts on 26th April.

In No. 2 Section, on 27th March, the 2nd Australian and New Zealand Army Corps came into existence on the departure of the 1st Australian and New Zealand Army Corps to France. The Corps was commanded by Lieut.-General Sir Alexander Godley, K.C.M.G., C.B., and consisted of the 4th Australian Division, commanded by Major-General Sir H. V. Cox, K.C.M.G., C.B., C.S.I., the 5th Australian Division, commanded by Major-General the Hon. J. MacCay, V.D., and the Anzac Mounted Division, commanded by Major-General H. G. Chauvel, C.B., C.M.G. (attached). In this section, the wells at Moiya Harab and Wadi um Muksheib having been brought into the regular patrolling area, a very successful reconnaissance to Bir el Jifjaffa was carried out between 11th and 15th April. The troops for this enterprise were a squadron of the 9th Australian Light Horse Regiment, accompanied by a detachment of Bikanir Camel Corps, and commanded by Major Scott, D.S.O., 9th Australian Light Horse. The objective was 52 miles from the starting point, and a jumping-off place for the attack, eight miles south-west of the objective, was reached at 2.30 a.m. on 13th April. From here an attack was launched by three troops upon the enemy's position at 9 a.m. The enemy, cut off in their attempted retreat by the right flanking party of the attack, stood at bay on one of the hills above the village, and lost six men killed and five wounded before surrendering. One Austrian lieutenant of engineers and 33 other prisoners were captured, our own casualties being one man and one horse killed. The destruction of the enemy's camp was thoroughly carried out, a quantity of correspondence was taken, and the elaborate well-boring plant, which had been at work for five months, was completely demolished. The manner in which this operation was carried out was most creditable both to the commander of the column, and to all ranks composing it.

In conjunction with this reconnaissance, a mounted column was sent out in No. 1 Section to reconnoitre Bir el Giddi and the roads leading east from it. This force satisfactorily accomplished its mission, and, after an encounter with a hostile patrol, captured unwounded three armed Arabs.

In the Katia District, where alone there is sufficient water supply to maintain a large body of troops, preliminaries to the accomplishment of our ultimate aim —the permanent occupation of the well-watered zone radiating 15 miles east and south-east of Katia—were steadily pushed on. On 2nd April, a squadron of the Gloucestershire Hussars under Lieut.-Colonel Yorke, with a detachment of Bikanir Camel Corps, reconnoitred Bir el Abd, some 15 miles east of Katia, met

FIRST DESPATCH

with no resistance, and burnt some tents and stores belonging to the enemy. On the following day, Bir el Mageibra, 10 miles south-east of Katia, was reconnoitred by the Worcestershire Yeomanry. On the 6th April, Brigadier-General E. A. Wiggin, commanding the 5th Mounted Brigade, took command of the Katia District, and was made responsible direct to the headquarters of No. 3 Section.

On 9th April, a further reconnaissance of Bir el Abd was undertaken by a squadron of Worcestershire Yeomanry. This time a strong party of enemy were found in possession of a ridge north-east of Bir el Abd. A sharp skirmish ensued when the Yeomanry attacked, and the enemy was driven eastwards from his position, but, owing to the heaviness of the sand, it was impossible for our cavalry to keep up the attack, and, after easily fending off an attempt at a flank attack, they withdrew unmolested. On 12th April, on orders being received for General Horne to proceed to France, Major-General the Hon. H. A. Lawrence took over the command of No. 3 Section, still retaining command of the 52nd Division. The 15th Army Corps at the same time ceased to exist.

By the 21st April, the railway towards Katia had reached a point upon which a serious advance to hold the whole district could be based, as soon as the necessary dispositions could be made. On the 23rd, however, the enemy attempted to forestall any such advance by making a sudden raid in force upon Katia. This operation, though comparatively small forces were engaged, produced the severest fighting yet experienced by the force under my command.

8. On 21st April, the 5th Mounted Brigade were disposed as follows :—the Worcestershire Yeomanry at

Katia, the Warwickshire Yeomanry, less one squadron, at Bir el Hamisah, three miles S.S.W. of Katia, and Brigade Headquarters and the Gloucestershire Yeomanry at Romani, six miles N.W. of Katia. General Wiggin, commanding the Brigade, had received orders to dispose his Brigade in the Katia District in such a manner as to protect all railway, topographical and water survey parties, with special attention to the exploitation of the water supply; also to observe the route eastwards towards Bir el Abd, but not to take any serious offensive measures without further orders. It had also been impressed on General Wiggin by the General Officer Commanding No. 3 Section, that, since it would take two days to reinforce him with infantry, he was, in the event of a heavy attack, to manœuvre back upon Bir el Dueidar, 13 miles from Kantara on the Katia road, or upon the rail-head near Bir el Arais, some seven miles N.W. of Katia. On the evening of the 21st, one squadron of Worcestershire Yeomanry moved into bivouac at Oghratina, seven miles E.N.E. of Katia, to cover an R.E. party detailed to prepare wells. On the 22nd another squadron of Worcestershire Yeomanry proceeded to Oghratina, being replaced in Katia by a squadron of Gloucestershire Yeomanry, pending the arrival of one regiment of the Anzac Mounted Division, which had been ordered up from Salihiya (see Map 2) so as to reach Katia on the 24th. The remainder of the 2nd Australian Light Horse Brigade was marching to arrive at Kantara on the 23rd.

In Katia the squadron of Gloucestershire Yeomanry was covered by good trenches for some 50 or 60 men, and a number of smaller shelters afforded good cover. Their horses were picketed close to their camp.

The officer commanding the two squadrons of

FIRST DESPATCH

Worcestershire Yeomanry at Oghratina had been told to push on entrenchment as far as possible, and it was General Wiggin's intention that these squadrons, if attacked in force, should retire on Katia and thence, if necessary, on Romani, with their left flank covered by the Gloucestershire Yeomanry and their right by the Warwickshire Yeomanry from Bir el Hamisah.

On the morning of the 23rd, both posts stood to arms at 4 a.m., and I have ascertained that patrols had gone out by that hour, though those at Oghratina were probably much hampered by a thick fog.

On the 22nd April the Royal Flying Corps reported to No. 3 Section that new bodies of enemy troops were at Bir el Bayud, 15 miles E.S.E. of Katia, and Bir el Mageibra, ten miles S.E. of Katia. Upon receipt of this information, General Wiggin obtained leave from General Officer Commanding No. 3 Section to attack the enemy at Bir el Mageibra that night, reporting that he intended to use two squadrons of Warwickshire, and the one remaining squadron of Worcestershire Yeomanry. General Wiggin, with Lieut.-Colonel Coventry, commanding the Worcestershire Yeomanry, accompanied the raid to Bir el Mageibra. Finding very few enemy, they destroyed the camp and returned to Bir el Hamisah about 9 a.m. on the 23rd with six Turkish prisoners. In the meantime the post at Oghratina was attacked at 5.30 a.m. This attack was repulsed. No further information was received from the officer commanding at Oghratina until 7 a.m., when he reported that he was again heavily attacked on all sides. This attack carried the post, all the garrison of which were either killed, wounded, or captured. No details of the fighting have, therefore, been obtainable. Katia itself was attacked about 9.30 a.m. Lieut.-Colonel Coventry was detached with one squadron of Worcestershire Yeomanry from General Wiggin's Force to operate towards Katia. Unfortunately, this squadron became involved in the unsuccessful resistance of the Katia Garrison, and, with the exception of some 60 men and one officer who were able to disengage themselves, fell with it into the hands of the enemy. I have therefore been able to gather no detailed information of the actual fighting at Katia.

General Wiggin and Colonel Yorke, commanding the Gloucestershire Yeomanry at Romani, both showed great judgment in dealing with the situation, and did all that was possible with their small forces against the enemy force of about 2,500 with four guns of small calibre. General Wiggin pushed forward from Hamisah north-east against the enemy's left, south of Um Ugba, and drove him back for about a mile; the advance was slow owing to the nature of the ground and the determined resistance encountered. Colonel Yorke, after hearing that Dueidar was safe, moved his whole force at 10 a.m. to attack the enemy's right advancing on Katia. He skilfully drove the Turkish right back to El Rabah, and caused their guns to shift their position further east. The enemy gave ground slowly, and, since by 3.30 p.m. it was evident that Katia had fallen, General Wiggin determined to fall back; he himself retired on Dueidar by way of Hamisah, Colonel Yorke on Romani: neither was followed. Meanwhile, at 5.30 a.m. a Turkish force 1,000 strong with one gun, advancing from the south, attacked Dueidar, the most advanced defensible post, which was held by 100 men of the 5th Battalion, Royal Scots Fusiliers, under the command of Captain Roberts, 5th Battalion, Royal

Scots Fusiliers. This officer, who throughout showed conspicuous skill and ability, succeeded in repelling two determined attacks on the position at 6.30 a.m. and 8.30 a.m. respectively. Both attempts cost the enemy dear. At 9.30 a.m. reinforcements of two companies, 4th Royal Scots Fusiliers, under the command of Major Thompson, 4th Battalion, Royal Scots Fusiliers, who had been despatched from Hill 70, seven miles away, on the first news of the attack, arrived at Dueidar. The various posts were strengthened, and a counter-attack, delivered at 12.30 p.m. with great spirit, forced the enemy to retire, leaving 30 prisoners in our hands and 70 dead. The Turks were pursued in their retreat by the 5th Australian Light Horse, who had only arrived at Kantara at 1 p.m., and by aeroplanes, thereby suffering further loss. Besides the three and a half squadrons of yeomanry and details lost at Katia and Oghratina, our casualties on the 23rd were 2 officers and 18 men killed, 4 officers and 21 men wounded. Aeroplane reconnaissance on the evening of the 23rd established the fact that the enemy force, which included a large body of picked Turkish regular troops, was already retiring. At dawn on the 24th, eight machines of the 5th Wing, Royal Flying Corps, made a bomb and machine-gun attack from a low altitude on the enemy troops left in Katia, causing very heavy casualties and completely destroying the camp. One machine also located and attacked a large body of enemy at Bir el Abd, and located another party retiring on Bir Bayud. On the morning of the 25th, further bomb and machine-gun attacks were made by the Royal Flying Corps on enemy forces at Bir el Abd and Bir Bayud. Both attacks were extremely successful, working great havoc among men and animals. I cannot speak too highly of the admirable work done by the 5th Wing, Royal Flying Corps, during these few days. The strain thrown on pilots and machines was very heavy, and the former displayed the utmost gallantry and resource on all occasions. Chiefly through their efforts the enemy was made to pay a very heavy price for his partially successful raid. The general situation in front of No. 3 Section was not affected by these operations. Our cavalry continued to patrol the Katia district, which was now practically clear of the enemy, while our infantry posts at Dueidar and Romani were strengthened, and the railway towards Romani was pushed on with all speed.

9. After 16th January, when General Sarrail assumed supreme control of the operations of the Allied Forces at Salonica, the British Force there, commanded by Lieut.-General Sir B. T. Mahon, K.C.V.O., C.B., D.S.O., only remained under my control for administrative purposes. From the beginning of January to the end of April, no active operations of importance took place. The general line of defences remained practically unaltered. Some 200 miles of deep trenches, including communication trenches, 710 emplacements for guns, 230 reduits or strong posts, 160 miles of obstacles (barbed wire) and 1,300 miles of telegraph cable have been completed; and the defences as a whole are now quite ready for occupation should the situation demand it.

On the 12th January, the railway bridge at Demir Hissar and smaller bridges near Kilindir were destroyed by the French. On the 28th January, Kara Burun Fort, covering the entrance to Salonica Harbour, was occupied by Allied troops, the Greek garrison merely protesting. During February, excepting two air raids, which caused considerable damage in the town and in the French main depôt, nothing of interest occurred. During March and April the French gradually pushed detachments forward towards the frontier, and by the end of April had, roughly, a brigade of cavalry, five or six brigades of infantry, and a proportion of artillery distributed along a line from about Snevce to about Kara Sinanci. Detachments of French troops were also posted at various points along the Monastir railway line; and British yeomanry squadrons were detached to near Orfano, to Orljak and to Kopriva. At General Sarrail's request, British troops took over a portion of this advanced line, namely that between the hills west of the Spanc valley on the right and the Sarigol-Doiran railway on the left. For this purpose the 7th Mounted Brigade, followed by an infantry and an artillery brigade, and later by a second infantry brigade, were employed. The headquarters of the British sector is at Kukus. Artillery duels and constant petty skirmishing have taken place with the enemy along the advanced line, and a number of prisoners and deserters have been taken. The Allied casualties have been very slight. Meanwhile the enemy forces have been mainly engaged in establishing a series of defensive works on their frontier line, on all possible lines of approach thereto, and on the coast; also in extensively improving their lines of communication in all directions, by which means the transport to the frontier of heavy artillery has become practicable. By the end of April, the total enemy forces, extending from Monastir to Xanthi, were about 8 Bulgarian divisions and 7 German regiments, or, roughly, 220,000 rifles. Along the Allied front between Huma and the Struma river, the frontier was continually crossed by small enemy detachments, some of which definitely established themselves over the frontier.

Since the deportation in December last of the enemy consuls and their adherents, the activity of enemy agents in and around Salonica has very sensibly diminished; but, so long as the administration of Salonica and the surrounding country remains in the hands of the Greeks, the position is a difficult one to grapple with. Increased pressure has, however, been brought to bear on the Greeks lately, and, in certain cases, the Allied authorities have assumed a more extensive control. More stringent measures, for instance, have been taken for the removal of undesirable persons from Salonica and for the restriction of traffic across the Allied defended zone. The enemy espionage organisations outside the zone of Allied occupation have been working with considerable vigour; but the capture, on the 27th April, by our yeomanry, of the German Consul at Drama, who was director of the enemy organisation in Macedonia, has had a restraining effect upon these hostile agencies.

As in Egypt, so in Salonica the administrative work has been extremely heavy. At the outset the state of the communications was very unsatisfactory. There were only two metalled roads leading to our lines, both in a shocking state of repair; the few existing tracks soon became impassable in wet weather for everything except pack animals. The construction and repair of roads had, therefore, to proceed simultaneously with the preparation of the defences. Roads in the forward area were all begun by the troops themselves, and all ranks worked admirably, the men thoroughly recognising the importance of the matter. Later, it was found possible to organise local civilian labour companies, who have largely been employed to complete and maintain the road work begun by the troops. Altogether about 90 miles of new metalled cart-roads have been constructed and 105 miles of mule-tracks, besides some 60 miles of repairs done to previously existing roads and tracks. Railway extensions leading to the various depôts on the Monastir road, with the necessary sidings, have been constructed, and Decauville lines laid within the depôts themselves. Preparations have been made for further extensions. Another great difficulty, that of insufficient wharfage accommodation, has been met by the construction of new piers in the bay itself and at Skala Stavros. These have reduced the congestion to an appreciable extent and fully justified the labour and expense involved.

The supply system, though hindered at first by the state of the communications and by the fact that the equipment of the force with a special scale of transport was only in process of gradual completion, has worked with uninterrupted success. The health of the troops has been excellent, all ranks having benefited by hard physical work in good climatic conditions. In view of the approach of summer, when malaria is likely to prevail in certain districts through which our line passes, special precautions have been taken for the protection of the troops, and, where possible, alternative positions prepared.

Throughout the period the importance of training the troops has been insisted upon. At first one day weekly was devoted to training as opposed to roadmaking or work on the defences. This proportion has gradually risen to four days weekly, excluding one day of rest. Two considerations have been kept in view throughout—the possibility of a return to ordinary trench warfare, and that of more open warfare in the Balkans. At the end of April General Mahon reported that discipline was good, that all ranks remained keen and cheerful and that in the first four months of this year the efficiency of the Salonica Army as a whole, including all services and departments, had been doubled.

On 9th May, under orders from the War Office, Lieut.-General G. F. Milne, C.B., D.S.O., succeeded Lieut.-General Sir Bryan Mahon, K.C.V.O., C.B., D.S.O., in command of the Salonica Army. General Mahon sailed on the same date to take up command of the Western Frontier Force in Egypt.

By 5th May the British detachment in advance of Salonica consisted of the 7th Mounted Brigade and the 22nd Division, the whole detachment being placed on this date under the command of Major-General the Hon. F. Gordon, C.B., D.S.O., Commanding 22nd Division. Nothing of importance occurred till 27th May, when an enemy force of all arms advanced across the frontier and occupied the Greek fortress of Rupel without opposition from the garrison. Subsequently the enemy occupied the high ground north and east of Demir Hissar, but have advanced no further. During the month the enemy have displayed increasing artillery activity from the direction of Doiran, but otherwise no active operations, except encounters between patrols, have taken place on the Salonica front.

10. Towards the end of April I was informed by the War Office that, in order to detain as many Turkish troops as possible on the coast of Asia Minor, steps had already been taken to give the enemy the impression that a large force was to be concentrated in Cyprus for landing operations in Syria or Asia Minor. I was

instructed, in consultation with the Naval authorities, to do what was possible to further this impression. I accordingly sent to Cyprus Major (temp. Lieut.-Colonel) H. Needham, then A.Q.M.G., 9th Army Corps, with two other staff officers, and the 22nd Garrison Battalion, The Rifle Brigade. My instructions to Lieut.-Colonel Needham—that by every possible means it should be made to appear that this was the advance party of a much larger force—were most efficiently carried out, and the objects of this feint were successfully attained.

Early in May the Royal Naval Division was ordered to proceed to France, and I received instructions to send two garrison battalions with certain artillery and engineer personnel to relieve this division in garrisoning the islands of Lemnos, Imbros and Tenedos. The 2nd Garrison Battalion, King's Liverpool Regiment, was sent from Egypt, and was joined later by the garrison battalion which had just completed its special mission in Cyprus. Brigadier-General F. W. B. Gray, C.M.G., D.S.O., was put in command of the islands, being under my orders for tactical purposes, and under the Salonica Army for administration.

11. In Egypt during the month of May there was no major operation to record. Intelligence received early in the month showed that the Turks had materially increased their numbers in Sinai, doubtless with the view of detaining troops in Egypt. The enemy's main concentrations were too far away for me to strike at them, and I was in hopes that he might be induced to cross the barrier of hills which extends from north to south some sixty miles from the Canal: he would then have been exposed to attack with the defiles behind him. However, he made no such advance, and,

during the hot weather in the middle of May there were indications that he was drawing in his advanced posts. On the 8th and 21st May, enemy aircraft attacked Port Said with bombs, doing no material damage. On the first occasion 3 civilians were wounded; on the second, 2 civilians were killed, 5 soldiers and 13 civilians were wounded. In each case the attack was answered by prompt and successful retaliation by the Royal Flying Corps. In all sections of the eastern front, reconnaissances were frequent, particularly in No. 3 Section, to which were now allotted three brigades of the Anzac Mounted Division. During the month the Mahemdia—Romani district has been occupied in some force, and at a conference held on 17th May, at which General Lawrence, commanding No. 3 Section, was present, further decisions regarding the occupation of the Katia district were arrived at. I considered that it would not be essential to carry and maintain a line of communication right through this district to its eastern limit, but that if the railway were pushed out to the latitude of Um Ugba, two miles east of Katia, and a strong defensive position were maintained in front of the rail-head, control of the eastern portion of the district could be satisfactorily maintained by our mobile troops operating from the advanced defensive position. General Lawrence was, therefore, instructed to prepare a strong defensive position, facing east, astride of the Katia—El Arish road, between Um Ugba and Hod el Reshafat, this position to be designed for about 4,000 infantry and sufficient mounted troops to ensure the effective control of the country to the east, as far as Bir el Abd. A second position, designed for 2,000 infantry and proportionate mounted troops, was to be selected and prepared by General Lawrence to cover

FIRST DESPATCH 35

Romani and Mahemdia. I also directed that the works at Dueidar were to be extended and improved to accommodate a garrison of between 500 and 1,000 infantry, and that the main railway line should be carried on from Romani to the rear of the advanced position near Um Ugba.

During the month several successful reconnaissances to the east were made by the Anzac Mounted Division, which proved itself a unit upon which I could absolutely depend to display energy, resource and endurance. On the 8th May, starting early from Oghratina, the 2nd Light Horse Brigade reconnoitred to Bir el Abd with patrols pushed out to Hod Salmana. On the 16th May, a day of intense heat, the same brigade, starting from Hod el Sagia, five miles E.S.E. of Katia, reached Hod el Bayud, 15 miles on in the same direction, at 7 a.m. Camels and dismounted men were seen making off in a north-easterly direction. The enemy's camp was destroyed, and one prisoner, 36 camels and a quantity of ammunition were brought in. The reconnaissance returned to Katia, having covered 60 miles in 30 hours. During this time the Canterbury Mounted Rifles went out to Bir Abu el Afein, covering 40 miles in 30 hours.

On the 18th May a very successful bombardment of El Arish from the sea and the air was carried out. A sloop and two monitors of His Majesty's Navy bombarded the town, reducing the fort S.W. of the town to ruins, and damaging the aerodrome. The seaplanes of the Royal Naval Air Service then attacked with bombs, being followed later by six machines of the Royal Flying Corps, who had orders to attack any enemy aircraft that appeared, and to bomb the enemy's camp and troops. The camps were effectively bombed, and three bombs exploded in the middle of a body of a thousand men who were on the march south of the town. A close reconnaissance of El Arish from the air was made, and many valuable photographs taken at the same time. All ships and aircraft returned safely. On 22nd May the Royal Flying Corps carried out a highly effective bombardment of all enemy camps on a 45-mile front, roughly parallel to the Canal, during which severe damage was done to the waterworks at Bir Rodh Salem, and to buildings at Bir el Hamma and Bir el Mazar. On 23rd May the 2nd Australian Light Horse Brigade reconnoitred Hod el Gedadia, 15 miles east of Katia, where shots were exchanged with a patrol of 40 men on camels, who retired. Finally, on 31st May, the New Zealand Mounted Rifles Brigade, one regiment of Australian Light Horse, and a sub-section of the Ayrshire Battery, R.H.A., attacked the enemy's post at Bir Salmana, 20 miles E.N.E. of Katia. The post was surrounded before dawn, and an enemy post on the Ganadil road was rushed, while a camel detachment was seen making off to the south-east. The enemy lost 15 men killed and two men captured. Our cavalry pursued till 8 a.m., when the pursuit was taken up by aeroplanes which bombed scattered parties with effect, killing 20 camels and 8 more men. The force returned, having covered 60 miles in 36 hours besides fighting an engagement. The only casualties were two men slightly wounded.

Towards the end of the month, orders having been received for the embarkation in June of the 4th and 5th Australian Divisions to France with the Headquarters of the 2nd Australian and New Zealand Army Corps, preparations were made to relieve them in No. 2 Section. One brigade of the 53rd Division was moved to this section, and I directed the General Officer Commanding 53rd Division to be prepared to assume command of No. 2 Section on the approaching departure of Lieut.-General Sir Alexander Godley.

On the western front during May, preliminary measures for the occupation of the Baharia Oasis have been in progress. A line of blockhouses has been established along the Darb el Rubi, which runs due west from Samalut on the Nile. Four blockhouses were completed and occupied by 23rd May. Work on the two remaining blockhouses has been postponed till the railway has reached a point where it can materially assist in the supply of stores; this should be about the end of June. From the most advanced blockhouse it is now possible to reconnoitre as far as the Mohariq sand-dunes, some 80 miles west of Samalut. The difficulty of maintaining such a line in a waterless desert subject to frequent and severe sand-storms has not been small, but all ranks have worked well and with great keenness.

The enemy has a small body of troops, under the command of Nuri, collected on the Libyan side of the frontier west of Sollum, but as yet he has not openly displayed his intentions. Two battalions of Italian troops landed at Moraisa (west of Sollum) during the month and have occupied Bardia. The relations between the Italian and British Commanders on the frontier are excellent, but military co-operation has been rendered difficult by the instructions of the Italian Government to the commander at Bardia. Negotiations are now in progress which, I hope, will remove the difficulties. The area between Sollum and Barrani (west of Sollum) has been cleared of the Bedouin population, and, though it has been impossible entirely to prevent communication between the Bedouins and

Siwa, the energy of our patrols, according to numerous reports, is successfully restricting the entry of food supplies into Siwa.

By means of patrols of Imperial Camel Corps and motor-cars, communication between the oases occupied by the enemy and the Nile Valley and Delta has been rendered almost impossible. In particular, the camel-patrolling from Kharga towards Dakhla and Beris has been carried out most efficiently by No. 1 Imperial Camel Company under especially trying conditions. The Farafra, Baharia, Moghara, and Wadi Natron fronts have also been controlled with great vigilance.

The Aulad Ali tribes in Egyptian territory are now all west of Barrani, except for a receiving camp at Sollum. Markets have been established for the sale of food at Sollum, Mersa Matruh, Dhabba, El Hammame, and Wadi Natron, where they are allowed to purchase what is necessary for their daily needs. This restricts indiscriminate movement to the west or to the Delta.

In spite of the occupation, during very hot weather, of so many advanced posts in the desert or on its edge, I am glad to report that the health of the troops has been remarkably good. I much regret, however, that General Sir Bryan Mahon, shortly after his arrival in this country to take up the command of the Western Frontier Force, had to be invalided home, owing to severe sunstroke. In the meantime Major-General A. G. Dallas, C.B., Commanding 53rd Division, has continued, with great ability, in temporary command of that force.

12. I beg to acknowledge, with great respect, the valuable assistance I have received from His Highness the Sultan of Egypt. He has with great kindness placed

FIRST DESPATCH

at my disposal his unrivalled knowledge of affairs affecting his country.

To His Excellency the High Commissioner, Lieut.-Colonel Sir A. H. McMahon, G.C.V.O., K.C.I.E., C.S.I., and to the Government of Egypt, I owe a deep debt of gratitude for whole-hearted co-operation and help.

I am very greatly indebted to Vice-Admiral Sir R. E. Wemyss, K.C.B., C.M.G., M.V.O., and the naval forces under his command for constant assistance and active co-operation.

The construction of roads, waterworks, and kindred tasks in connection with the Canal Defences, which I have described to you, owe their accomplishment, in a very large measure, to the admirable services of Colonel Sir Murdoch Macdonald, K.C.M.G., of the Public Works Department of Egypt. His wide experience and capacity have been an indispensable asset to me in dealing with these important problems.

I am particularly indebted to the Railway Department, under Colonel Sir George Macauley, K.C.M.G., Reserve of Officers, Royal Engineers, for the highly successful manner in which railway communication has been carried on under great difficulties. The movement of a large number of troops and impedimenta of an army has severely taxed the capacity of the railway, and has put a great strain on its staff. That it never failed to accomplish what was desired is due to the high efficiency this department has attained, and to the personal exertions of Colonel Sir George Macauley.

I wish to bring to your notice the very responsible and important duties that have fallen to my Director of Army Signals, Brigadier-General M. G. E. Bowman-

Manifold, D.S.O., R.E., and to the admirable way in which he has discharged them.

Military operations on the two fronts have been spread over a very wide front, amounting to close on 1,000 miles in the west and 90 miles in the east. Prompt and reliable intercommunication has been a matter of vital importance.

In the successful achievement of this I beg also to bring to your notice the services of the Egyptian Telegraph Department, under Lieut.-Colonel J. S. Liddell, D.S.O., Royal Engineers, and to express my thanks to the Eastern Telegraph Company and the Telephone Company of Egypt, who have given my Director of Army Signals unceasing valuable help.

I beg to bring to notice the valuable services rendered to the Canal Defences by the representative and principal officer of the Suez Canal Company, Charles, Comte de Serionne, Agent Supérieur de la Compagnie du Canal de Suez, and by the staff of that Company.

The arduous and important work of the care of the sick and wounded in the Hospitals has been considerably lightened by a large amount of voluntary aid. I wish specially to mention the work of the British Red Cross Society and Order of St. John of Jerusalem, under Sir Courtauld Thomson, C.B.

The Nursing Services, both English and Australian, have done admirable work, and the voluntary aid of the Sisters of Notre Dame de la Délivrance, working at the Austrian Hospital at Alexandria, has been specially brought to my notice.

Finally, and in conclusion, I wish to bring to notice the admirable services of my Chief of the General Staff, Major-General A. L. Lynden-Bell, C.B., C.M.G., my Deputy Quartermaster-General, Major-General W.

FIRST DESPATCH

Campbell, C.B., D.S.O., and my Deputy Adjutant-General, Major-General J. Adye, C.B. No Commander-in-Chief has ever been more loyally served and no staff has ever worked with less friction.

I have other names to bring to notice for distinguished and gallant service during the operations under review, and these will form the subject of a separate communication.

    I have the honour to be, Sir,
        Your most obedient servant,
            (Signed) A. J. MURRAY, General,
                  Commander-in-Chief,
                Egyptian Expeditionary Force.

SECOND DESPATCH
1st October, 1916

LIEUTENANT-GENERAL THE HON. H. A. LAWRENCE

SECOND DESPATCH

From—

    THE COMMANDER-IN-CHIEF,
        Egyptian Expeditionary Force.

To—

    THE SECRETARY OF STATE FOR WAR,
        War Office, London, S.W.

General Headquarters,
Egyptian Expeditionary Force,
1st October, 1916.

SIR,

I have the honour to submit a report on the operations of the Force under my command from the 1st June to the 30th September, 1916.

1. On the eastern front during the month of June, vigorous counter-measures, culminating in the successful attack on the enemy's aerodrome at El Arish, were undertaken to check the much increased activity of hostile aircraft. This operation was brilliantly carried out on the morning of the 18th June by 11 machines. Two of the machines, carrying observers, were ordered to fly in observation at a height of 7,000 feet ready to engage hostile aircraft, while the nine single-seaters were to attack the sheds from 600 feet. The enemy was completely surprised, owing to the fact that our machines, having kept well out to sea, wheeled five miles N.N.W. of El Arish, and delivered their attack from a south-easterly direction. The first British machine to arrive descended to 100 feet and attacked, blowing to pieces an aeroplane on the ground and its

attendant personnel. A second machine on the ground was also put out of action by bombs. Heavy fire from rifles and anti-aircraft guns was now opened on the attackers, but the British pilots carried out their orders most gallantly. Altogether six out of the ten hangars were hit, and two, if not three, were burnt to the ground. A party of soldiers on the aerodrome was also successfully bombed, and at the close one of the observing machines attacked the hangars with its machine gun from a height of 1,200 feet. During the action three of our machines were forced to descend; two were destroyed, and one sank in the sea. Two of the pilots were rescued, and the third was taken prisoner.

On the eastern front there was comparatively little activity during the month of June beyond the usual patrols and reconnaissances, which were actively carried out. In No. 2 Section a column of Australian Light Horse, with detachments of engineers and of Bikanir Camel Corps, under the command of Lieut.-Colonel T. J. Todd, D.S.O., successfully executed the task of draining the rock cisterns and pools in the Wadi um Muksheib, some 40 miles S.E. of Ismailia, between 10th and 14th June. Some 5,000,000 gallons of water were disposed of in four days and nights of continuous effort, and the fact that every man and animal that left rail-head on 10th June returned safely testifies to the efficiency of the staff arrangements. A column of Middlesex Yeomanry from No. 1 Section co-operated with this force and did very good work.

2. On the departure of the Headquarters, 2nd Australian and New Zealand Army Corps, to France, the command of No. 2 Section was taken over by Major-General A. G. Dallas, C.B.; and, on the receipt of instructions to embark the 11th Division for France

SECOND DESPATCH

after the 4th and 5th Australian Divisions, I formed a new section of the eastern front, numbered 2a, extending from the northern boundary of No. 2 Section to a line running east of Kilometre 50 on the Canal. The command of this section was taken over on 25th June by Major-General Sir W. Douglas, K.C.M.G., C.B. On 24th August the troops in No. 2a Section were put under the command of the General Officer Commanding, No. 3 Section, and No. 2a Section ceased to exist.

In No. 3 Section the Australian and New Zealand Mounted Division continued to do excellent work. On 10th and 11th June, Bir Bayud, Bir el Mageibra, and Bir el Jefeir were reconnoitred. Enemy stores and huts were destroyed at Hod el Bayud, and at Hod Abu Dhababis a hostile patrol was successfully disposed of. On 15th June, Bir el Abd was reconnoitred, and between 21st and 23rd June a reconnaissance of the Hod el Ge'eila, Hod um el Dhaunnin and Hod el Mushalfat area was carried out by the 1st Australian Light Horse Brigade. During the latter operation one of our aeroplanes was reported missing and the reconnoitring troops were ordered to find it. This they successfully accomplished, after considerable prolonged exertion in trying weather conditions, and the damaged engine and the machine gun were brought in on the 23rd. Bir el Abd and Bir el Mageibra were reconnoitred on 30th June and found to be clear of the enemy. On 27th June one division moved out to the entrenched camp at Mahemdia, and I obtained your sanction for the appointment of Major-General the Hon. H. A. Lawrence to the independent command of No. 3 Section with a small headquarters, and for his succession in command of his division by Major-General W. E. B. Smith, C.M.G.

In No. 1 Section at the beginning of July a small

reconnaissance was carried out from Abu Zeneima by detachments of the 23rd Sikh Pioneers and the Bikanir Camel Corps under the command of Major W. J. Ottley, 23rd Sikh Pioneers. The column left Abu Zeneima on 11th July and returned on 14th July, having captured an Arab sheik and some other prisoners.

3. As regards the western front, on 20th June Major-General Sir Charles Dobell, K.C.B., C.M.G., D.S.O., assumed command of the Western Frontier Force. During the month no important enemy movements took place on this front. In the coastal section, reconnaissances by aeroplane, motor and camel corps, to assure the safety of the Sollum post, were carried out irrespective of frontier, and with the agreement of the Italian local military authorities, with whom a complete accord has been established by the interchange of visits between the respective commanders. Progress on the Baharia railway continued, though slower than was anticipated, and the defences of posts in the Kharga oasis were completed. Aeroplane reconnaissance established the continued presence of an enemy force of some 1,800 rifles in the Dakhla oasis. On 25th and 26th July a raid from Sollum was carried out by a detachment of light armoured cars, under the command of Captain C. G. Mangles, 20th Hussars, in conjunction with some motor-cars and personnel furnished by the Italian garrison of Bardia, supported by half of No. 2 Company, Imperial Camel Corps, and by the Italian armed yacht *Misurata*, ably commanded by Captain Como, Italian Navy. The objective was a party of some 100 Muhafzia located near the mouth of the Wadi Sanal in Italian territory, 40 miles west of Ras el Melh, whence they had been robbing the Bedouins under pretence of collecting taxes for the

Senoussi. A complete surprise was effected, but only about 25 Muhafzia were found in camp. These fled towards the sea after a slight resistance, leaving six killed and three prisoners. Scattered groups on the sea-shore came under the gun-fire of the *Misurata*. The importance of this well-conducted operation lies in the proof which it gave to the Arabs of the close co-operation and good-fellowship that existed between our Italian neighbours and ourselves.

4. The end of June marked a definite stage in the existence of the Egyptian Expeditionary Force. During the month the 4th and 5th Australian Divisions, with the Headquarters of the 2nd Australian and New Zealand Army Corps, had been embarked for France, and the embarkation of the 11th Division, also for France, was nearly completed. The rôle of this force as a general strategic reserve for the Empire was practically at an end, for it had been reduced to the smallest strength compatible with securing the safety of Egypt during the summer months. In the first half of the year two complete divisions had been formed, equipped and trained; six divisions had been either re-equipped or completed with equipment; three Territorial divisions and three brigades of dismounted yeomanry had been re-equipped for service in Egypt, and transport for two divisions had been collected on a special scale—all this in addition to the preparation of defences, the maintenance of the troops, the formation of brigade machine-gun companies, the raising of new personnel for the Camel Transport Corps, and new units for the Imperial Camel Corps, the continuous pushing forward of railways and improvement of water-supply, and attendance on the special needs of the Salonica Army. The total number of troops, including all the 11th Division, sent

out of the country was some 232,000 men, not including medical units or sick and wounded evacuated. In this total were comprised nine complete divisions and three independent infantry brigades, about 209,000 in all, besides some 11,000 Indian troops sent to the East, and nine batteries of heavy artillery.

The original scheme of defence, designed during the winter, 1915/16, to meet a heavy attack at any point, in positions prepared for occupation by 250,000 men, had already been considerably modified in the spring of this year, when the first large withdrawal of troops from Egypt, and the approach of summer, led me to remodel my dispositions on the basis of an outpost-line, lightly held and designed principally to cover the concentration and preliminary action of mobile reserves held in readiness in the neighbourhood of the Canal for offensive employment against an enemy advancing from the east. By July, however, the withdrawal of three more divisions, and the consequent reduction of the force available on the eastern front to four weak Territorial divisions, two weak Indian brigades, and a few garrison battalions (some 60,000 rifles), in addition to one mounted division and a mounted yeomanry brigade, made a further and final readjustment of my defensive measures in that zone necessary. During the hot weather it was exceedingly unlikely that any large enemy force could attack my centre or southern sections: in these sections, therefore, my policy was to be in readiness to attack any enemy column which should debouch on the western side of the rocky defiles which face those sections. In the northern section, however, my chief concern was the preparation of an active offensive towards El Arish, to take place as soon as possible in the autumn, with the objects of forestalling any Turkish attack along the northern road in the winter, and of securing an advantageous position on the enemy's flank, should he attack by the central road. Plans were accordingly prepared for purely defensive action in the southern and centre sections (*i.e.*, south of Ballah), with a view to developing my maximum strength for an active operation in the northern section, against which any advance by the enemy during the summer months would necessarily be directed owing to vital considerations of water-supply. This scheme allowed for the rapid concentration in No. 3 Section of two infantry divisions complete with attached troops, the Australian and New Zealand Mounted Division with the 5th Mounted Brigade attached, with full proportion of artillery. In addition, alternative plans were worked out in detail, whereby either (*a*) a general reserve of three infantry brigades could be created at twenty-four hours' notice, by withdrawing troops from the two remaining sections, without essential modification of the existing scheme of defence; or (*b*) a reserve of 19 infantry battalions, one yeomanry regiment, 10 R.F.A. 18-pounder and three howitzer batteries could be concentrated at forty-eight hours' notice. Since the latter alternative would entail withdrawal in No. 1 and No. 2 Sections practically to the line of bridge-heads and specially important points, it was my intention only to adopt it as a temporary measure and in circumstances of extreme urgency.

The prospective advance eastwards over the northern portion of the Sinai desert differed from any previous desert operations on a considerable scale in that it has to be undertaken without the benefit of the months, or even years, of preparation which have in the past—notably in the late Lord Kitchener's Sudan campaigns

—laid the groundwork for successful operations of this kind. For the force under my command, if it was to carry out this advance, the construction of roads and railways to provide rapid communication to the rear, the purchase of a very large number of camels to give mobility to the forward troops, and, above all, the provision of an adequate water-supply at points far out in the desert were questions just as urgent as the formulation and execution of the tactical plan. The water question was especially pressing, since the stretch of desert east of Kantara was, for our purposes, practically waterless. The saline water of the local wells, though tolerable to the Bedouin and even to the Turk, is, as a rule, only a source of sickness to European soldiers; and European animals, even if they will drink it, rapidly lose condition if restricted to this water alone. The main essential, therefore, of any preliminary advance during the dry weather was to secure an adequate delivery of fresh water as far east as the troops were likely to advance. It was calculated that for the final advance a supply of 500,000 gallons of water a day would be needed, and, for this purpose, all material was ordered, and contracts made, for the erection of a filter-plant at Kantara capable of supplying 600,000 gallons of filtered water a day, the construction of reinforced concrete reservoirs at Kantara and Romani with a capacity of 500,000 gallons each, the supply of enough 12-inch, 10-inch and 8-inch piping to carry the water within striking distance of El Arish and the provision of high-power oil engines for pumping the water from one fortified post to the next. The quick handling of all this heavy piping and machinery necessitated a large amount of preparatory work, including the construction of a new wharf with cranes

SECOND DESPATCH 53

and railway sidings at Kantara, and laid a very considerable burden upon the railways on the east bank of the Canal. Besides these preparations for the final advance, the immediate supply of water to the Romani district had to be considerably improved, so that a large body of troops could take up positions well in advance of Romani. The installation of a new and more powerful pump-house at Kantara and the construction of a 50,000-gallon reservoir and a condensing plant at Mahemdia, were among the measures taken to meet this necessity. The difficulties connected with the water-supply may be judged from the fact that, during the Turkish attack at the beginning of August, when it was still necessary to rely entirely on the water pumped from the filter-plant at Kantara and on that brought by water-boats along the Canal, an accidental fire in the engine-house of the filter-plant nearly caused the entire breakdown of the water-supply system on this section; this serious danger was only averted by the resource and energy of the local engineer staff. Since that time the local reservoirs have been completed, and the Royal Engineer units with the fighting troops have been specially organised for the purpose of developing and improving the water-supply from the local wells and springs.

The main railway east from Kantara, the construction of which was essential to any permanent advance, has proceeded since the end of May as fast as the supply of material and the exigencies of other engineering work in the northern section allowed. The advance of the Turks in the latter half of July necessitated the stoppage of work on this line for 24 days, and the construction of a metre-gauge railway from Gilban to Dueidar, a distance of six miles. This latter work had to be completed in great haste, together with the laying of some miles of 5-inch and 4-inch water-piping, at a time when the railways were working at high pressure in moving troops, ammunition, and supplies.

The energy with which these heavy and multifarious labours were carried out by the engineer staff, the officers and men of the Royal Engineers, and by the Egyptian Labour Corps, admirably organised by the Inspector-General of Communications and ably officered by gentlemen residing in Egypt, calls for the highest praise. The work of the railway transport officers and the officers and men responsible for running the railways is equally deserving of commendation. In this connection my thanks are especially due to my late Engineer-in-Chief, Major-General G. Williams, and to my present Engineer-in-Chief, Major-General H. B. H. Wright, C.M.G., late R.E., the Director of Railways, Colonel Sir G. Macauley, K.C.M.G., R. of O., Lieut.-Colonel G. Lubbock, R.E., who has been in charge of railway construction, and Brigadier-General E. McL. Blair, R.E., Chief Engineer of No. 3 Section.

With regard to the supply of camels, the liberal provision of which would normally have been an indispensable preliminary to any such operations, I have been hampered by the necessity of buying at an unfavourable time of year, so that the demands of this force have always been in excess of the supply. I am most grateful for the assistance given me by the Sirdar in the collection of camels.

5. More than half the month of July passed without any important occurrence on the eastern front. In the northern section the Australian and New Zealand Mounted Division carried out frequent reconnaissances to the east, penetrating on 9th July as far as Salmana,

but found the country clear of all but a few Bedouins. On 17th July, however, enemy aircraft were active over the Romani—Dueidar area, and on the 18th a patrol of the 2nd Australian Light Horse Brigade came in contact with a camel patrol of 15 Turks, with whom shots were exchanged. The Turks retired rapidly eastwards. Up till this date there was no considerable body of Turkish troops further west than Bir el Mazar, some 18 miles east of Oghratina, where for some time there had been a camp of between 1,500 and 2,000.

The situation suddenly changed on July 19th, when an evening reconnaissance by the Royal Flying Corps revealed the fact that a large force of the enemy had moved westwards from El Arish and established itself on the line Bir el Abd—Bir Jameil—Bir Bayud. Their numbers were estimated to be between 8,000 and 9,000, of which from 3,000 to 4,000 were at Bir el Abd, and the remainder divided between the other two places. It was not immediately clear whether the enemy's intention was to repeat the raid of 23rd April on the Katia district on a larger scale, or to make a more deliberate advance, but I at once decided, on receipt of this information, to reinforce the troops in No. 3 Section. The 158th Brigade of the 53rd Division, then in General Reserve at Moascar (near Ismailia), moved to Kantara on the night of the 19th/20th, being replaced in General Reserve by four battalions from Nos. 1 and 2 Sections, and the 127th Brigade was completed by the move of its two remaining battalions from El Ferdan. On 20th July the machine-gun companies of the 127th, 160th, and 161st Brigades were also ordered to No. 3 Section, with a detachment of Stokes guns and No. 3 Armoured Train. The troops resting at Sidi Bishra (see inset, Alexandria, Map 2), which included two battalions of the 156th

Brigade, were ordered to return to their sections. On the night of the 19th/20th the General Officer Commanding, No. 3 Section, reinforced Romani by the 156th Brigade (less two battalions) with two battalions of the 127th Brigade attached. Major-General Chauvel, commanding Australian and New Zealand Mounted Division, who had one brigade bivouacked at Katia, was ordered to send out patrols before daylight on the 20th to get into touch with the enemy and to keep his brigades concentrated in readiness for a reconnaissance in force.

Early on the morning of the 20th the cavalry reported that Oghratina was held by strong forces of the enemy who were entrenching. This was confirmed by the Royal Flying Corps, who further reported that the pile of stores at Bir el Abd had increased in size, and that the troops reported on the previous evening at Bir Jameil and Bir Bayud had moved. A further air reconnaissance, in the afternoon, revealed that this force had moved to Bir el Mageibra, where there were between 2,000 and 3,000 men, with bodies of between 500 and 600 moving on a line between that place and Oghratina. The General Officer Commanding, Australian and New Zealand Mounted Division, was instructed to keep his horses as fresh as possible at this stage, and both he and the General Officer Commanding, 52nd Division, were instructed to allow the enemy to involve himself in an attack on our defences, if he would, and not to hinder any such intention by a premature counter-attack. The cavalry were in touch with the enemy all day, capturing a few prisoners, from whose information it appeared that the force in front of us was the 3rd Turkish Division, consisting of the 31st, 32nd, and 39th Regiments, with mountain guns, heavy artillery, and special machine-gun companies; the artillery was manned by Turks, Germans, and Austrians, and there were Germans with all the machine-gun companies. Prisoners also stated that there were other echelons following behind these advanced troops at a distance of one day's march. This information was confirmed in all essentials by the completer knowledge subsequently obtained of the attacking force, except that prisoners all exaggerated the number of troops that was following behind them. The whole force consisted of the Turkish 3rd Division, with eight machine-gun companies officered and partly manned by Germans, mountain artillery, and some batteries of 4-inch and 6-inch howitzers and anti-aircraft guns, manned chiefly by Austrians, with a body of Arab camelry. It was commanded by Colonel Kress von Kressenstein, a German officer in Turkish employ, and the German personnel of the machine-gun units, heavy artillery, wireless sections, field hospital and supply section had been organised in Germany as a special formation for operations with the Turkish forces. The force was in fine physical condition and admirably equipped.

On the evening of the 20th, a demonstration with artillery against Oghratina disclosed the fact that the enemy was entrenching on a general line running south-east from Oghratina, with his left flank thrown forward to Bir el Mageibra, which was strongly held. Bir el Abd was used by the enemy as an advanced base throughout the operations.

During the next few days there was no appreciable change in the situation. The enemy confined himself to closing up his troops and strengthening the position already occupied, pushing forward in one or two places and entrenching wherever he established himself. There were constant encounters between our cavalry patrols and the enemy's, but the latter handled his covering troops well, and extended his right flank far enough northwards to prevent anything less than a very strong attack from interfering with his communications along the Bir el Abd—Oghratina road.

By the 24th, the enemy had established a force, estimated at 5,000 men, in a series of entrenched positions extending from Hod el Negiliat through Oghratina to Hod el Masia, with supporting bodies of about 1,000 each at Bir Abu el Afein and Bir el Abd behind his right flank. On his left, Bir el Mageibra was entrenched with a series of strong redoubts and held by some 3,000 troops, with small connecting posts northward to Hod el Masia.

By 22nd July it was evident that the enemy had no intention of making an immediate raid upon the Katia district, but was either contemplating a serious attack upon the Canal Defences further west, or preparing to establish himself firmly in the Um Aisha district, so as to block our further advance towards El Arish, to protect his own communications between Syria and the Hedjaz (see Map 1) and to prevent us from denying to him the whole of the Katia area—the only district within which he could collect and maintain any considerable force within striking distance of the Suez Canal. In either case, whether, on the first alternative, he was waiting for further echelons to arrive before attacking, or, on the second, he was preparing to establish himself permanently, there was only one course of action that commended itself to me—namely, to attack the enemy and inflict a decisive defeat upon him as soon as possible. To do this forthwith was impracticable, since 15 miles of desert separated my main defensive position from that of the enemy, and it would be absolutely necessary that any force destined to advance across this tract

SECOND DESPATCH

to an attack on a strong enemy position should be equipped with camel transport on a very complete scale. While I was compelled, therefore, to remain for the moment on the tactical defensive, I took immediate steps to put everything in train for the adoption of a vigorous offensive at the earliest possible moment. On 24th July the 42nd Division was placed under the command of the General Officer Commanding, No. 3 Section, and the 3rd Australian Light Horse Brigade from No. 2 Section was also transferred to No. 3 Section. Schemes were also prepared whereby further troops could be withdrawn at very short notice from Nos. 1 and 2 Sections. The General Officer Commanding, No. 3 Section, was instructed to formulate his plan for the earliest possible assumption of the offensive, and to proceed with all speed with the mobilisation of his striking force on a pack basis with camel transport. I calculated that all arrangements would be completed during the first days of August, and this calculation was borne out by events. By 1st August, 10,500 transport camels had been concentrated in No. 3 Section, and by 3rd August all the formations were ready to take the field. My intention was to attack the enemy in force about 13th August, the date of full moon, unless myself attacked earlier.

During this period of energetic preparation the Australian and New Zealand Mounted Troops kept in constant touch with the enemy, harassing him in every possible way, and making valuable reconnaissances; and the Royal Flying Corps, having concentrated all available machines and pilots in Egypt on the eastern front, was able to make valuable reports upon the enemy's movements in rear of his advanced line.

On the night of the 27th/28th the enemy pushed

forward all along his front and occupied a line, in advance of his former entrenched position, running from the eastern end of Hod Amoia on the north, south-eastwards to Abu Darem on the south. On his right the advance was small, for his advanced troops, which at one time advanced to Hod um Ugba, were driven back after a sharp skirmish by the Canterbury Mounted Rifles, the enemy sustaining heavy losses. The chief advance was made by his left flank, which swung up in a north-westerly direction from Mageibra to Abu Darem. It now seemed likely that the enemy meant to attack, but for the next few days he continued strengthening his new positions, while continued reinforcements were observed to be reaching him along the northern road. This movement of reinforcements ceased on 31st July, by which date the enemy appeared to have completed the concentration of troops in his front line. From 29th July onwards, the Royal Flying Corps, whose rôle had hitherto been only one of observation, passed to the offensive, and constantly harassed the enemy with bomb attacks. From the 30th onwards H.M. Monitors M.15 and M.21, lying off Mahemdia, rendered most valuable assistance in shelling the enemy's camps and works, in which the Royal Flying Corps successfully co-operated. On 28th July I gave instructions to the General Officer Commanding, No. 2 Section, for the formation of a mobile column, under the command of Lieutenant-Colonel C. L. Smith, V.C., Imperial Camel Corps, to operate from the north of No. 2 Section against the enemy's left flank and left rear in the neighbourhood of Mageibra and Bayud respectively. This column, which was organised to operate in the desert as a complete unit for several successive days, consisted of Nos. 4, 6, 9 and 10 Companies Imperial Camel

Corps, Headquarters and two squadrons 1/1st City of London Yeomanry, Headquarters and two squadrons 11th Australian Light Horse Regiment, with special mobile engineering, medical and signal units; arrangements for its supply, watering and concentration were put in hand forthwith. This mobile column proved itself invaluable in subsequent operations.

The organisation of the troops in No. 3 Section on a mobile basis was rapidly nearing completion, and on 1st August the dispositions in that section were as follows:

Locality.	Formations.	Cavalry.	Infantry.	Guns.
Mahemdia—Romani	A. and N.Z. Mtd. Div. (less 2 brigades) 52nd Division 158th Brigade	3,000	11,000	36 (including 4 60-pdr.)
Dueidar	5th Australian Light Horse Regt. 1 Regt. Scottish Horse	500	500	—
Gilban	1 squadron Yeomanry 1 brigade, 42nd Division	100	3,500	4
Hill 70	New Zealand Mtd. Rifles Bde. 5th Mtd. Brigade 1 brigade, 42nd Division 1st Dismounted Bde. (500 only)	2,500	3,500	12
Hill 40	1 brigade, 42nd Division (less 1 battalion) 1st Dismounted Bde. (less 500)	—	5,000	—
Kantara	1 battalion, 42nd Division Artillery, 42nd and 52nd Divisions	—	700	48
Bally Bunion (Railhead E. of Ballah)	3rd Australian Light Horse Brigade	1,800	—	4

Two battalions of the 54th Division and the 15th Heavy Battery were also sent up from No. 1 Section. Lieut.-General the Hon. H. A. Lawrence, in command of No. 3 Section, directed the operations. The Mahemdia—Romani position consisted of a series of strong posts extending southwards from the sea to a point on the east of the Katib Gannit hill, and thence curving backwards round the southern slope of that hill northwestwards toward Bir Etmaler. In planning the occupation of these lines I had always contemplated the advantages to be gained by leaving a gap between Katib Gannit and Dueidar, which might induce the enemy to get involved in the dune country to the south and south-west, and oblige him to attack under very disadvantageous conditions as regards terrain. The main strength of the force was therefore concentrated in the Romani lines, the remainder being disposed in echelon in positions along the road from Dueidar to Kantara, from which it was possible to reinforce the Romani lines by the railway running from Kantara to Pelusium Station, about five miles due east of Romani. General Lawrence's instructions to the General Officer Commanding, 42nd Division, were that this Division, less one brigade retained in reserve by General Lawrence, should, in the event of an attack, be prepared either to move up the railway line and co-operate in an attack on the enemy's southern flank from Pelusium, or, if the enemy attacked from Dueidar, to repel the attack in conjunction with troops operating from the Hill 70 line.

On 2nd August, the General Officer Commanding, 42nd Division, was ordered to send forward a battalion to prepare a position in the neighbourhood of Pelusium Station to cover the detrainment and assembly of one

SANDHILLS SOUTH OF ROMANI

or both of the brigades under his command in that neighbourhood. On that day the 5th Mounted Brigade was also ordered to Gilban and placed under the orders of the General Officer Commanding, 42nd Division. As regards the 3rd Australian Light Horse Brigade, my intention was that it should move on the right of the New Zealand Mounted Rifles Brigade, south of the Bir el Nuss—Dueidar road.

On 2nd August there were indications of a forward move on the part of the enemy, who made a strong reconnaissance towards El Rabah—Katia and Bir el Hamisah, but his advanced troops were driven in, except on the north, by the Australian and New Zealand Mounted Division after some sharp encounters. By the evening of the 2nd August his general position was but little altered. Even up to this time it was still uncertain whether the ultimate assumption of the offensive would come from our side or the enemy's, but on the following day the enemy disclosed his intention of taking the initiative by making a general move forward and occupying a semicircular line running from the immediate west of Hill 110, past the high ground north-west of Rabah, over the high ground east and south-east of Katia to the high ground north-west of Bir el Hamisah. It then appeared certain that he would attack the Mahemdia—Romani position, and it appeared to me extremely probable that, while holding us east of that position, he would throw his main attack against the Katib Gannit—Bir el Nuss line in a north-westerly direction, with the object of forcing back our entrenched line before we could interfere from the west and north-west. I warned General Lawrence of this possibility, which was confirmed by events. The 160th Brigade was at once sent to No. 3 Section to free all mobile troops for action, and arrangements already made for replacing it in No. 2 Section were put into force. General Lawrence instructed the General Officer Commanding, 42nd Division, to move the remainder of the 127th Brigade to Pelusium as rolling-stock became available, to follow it with the 125th Brigade on the 4th, and to move forthwith the 5th Mounted Brigade by road to Pelusium.

6. On the night of the 3rd/4th August, owing to the proximity of the enemy at Katia, the cavalry, in addition to leaving out the usual officers' patrols, put out a strong outpost line which extended from just south of Katib Gannit along the entrance to the gullies between the sand dunes up to and including Hod el Enna, thus preventing the enemy from penetrating unobserved into the waterless area of sand dunes southwest of Romani, into which I anticipated he would attempt to move. This outpost line, formed by two regiments of the 1st Australian Light Horse Brigade, was attacked by the enemy in increasing strength from midnight onwards. Several attempts to force the line were repulsed, a bayonet charge on Mount Meredith, a high sand dune midway between Katib Gannit and Hod el Enna, being beaten off between 2 a.m. and 3 a.m. The continuous pressure of the enemy gradually forced back the outpost line, which by 4.20 a.m. was facing generally south along the dune called Wellington Ridge, between Mount Meredith and Katib Gannit. The 2nd Australian Light Horse Brigade extended on the right of the 1st Light Horse Brigade, but before long the enemy's threat to outflank our right made it necessary to retire slowly northwards towards the railway. It was evident by daylight that the enemy had committed his troops to a decisive attack, as he was

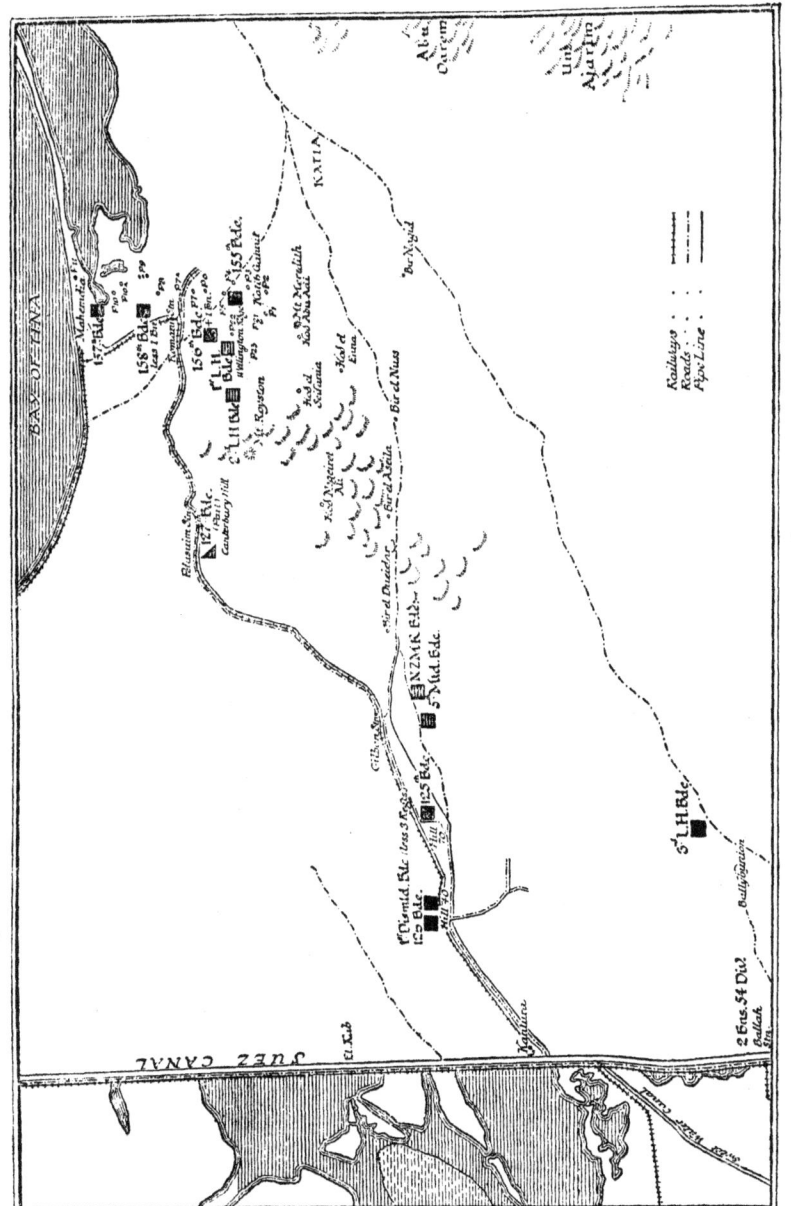

BATTLE OF ROMANI

Sketch Map showing Positions of British Troops at 6 a.m., 4th August, 1916

pressing the line of fortified works from the east, under cover of artillery fire from field-guns and heavy howitzers, at the same time as he was moving round the southern flank of the position with strong forces, before which our cavalry, while stubbornly resisting, were slowly retiring.

The situation had developed in accordance with my anticipations, and it was certain that, once the force of the enemy's attack from the south was spent, a decisive and rapid counter-attack would place him in a position of great difficulty. General Lawrence issued orders to the General Officer Commanding, 42nd Division, to be ready to operate with all available troops against the enemy's southern flank in the direction of Mount Royston, a high sand dune about two miles south of Pelusium Station; the New Zealand Mounted Rifles were directed to act vigorously from Dueidar towards Hod el Enna; the 3rd Australian Light Horse Brigade were ordered to send one regiment to Hod el Aras, and to be prepared to follow it up with the whole brigade, so as to co-operate with the New Zealand Mounted Brigade; finally, I issued orders to the Mobile Column under Lieut.-Colonel Smith, V.C., to commence operations against the enemy's left rear towards Mageibra and Bir el Aweidiya, working wide of the flank of the 3rd Australian Light Horse Brigade. This column at once started for Hod el Bada, which it reached by the evening of the 4th.

During the forenoon the enemy made several attacks against the Mahemdia—Romani defences from the east, south and south-west. These were repulsed by the garrisons, found by the 155th and 158th Infantry Brigades, with considerable loss, and in spite of heavy artillery fire from the enemy's heavy howitzers, which, in one or two cases, inflicted severe casualties on our troops, who behaved with admirable steadiness. The fire of these howitzers, however, was very effectively kept down by the guns of the monitors, with the co-operation of the Royal Flying Corps.

There was, unfortunately, more delay than had been anticipated in moving the infantry of the 42nd Division up to Pelusium Station, so that, during the morning of the 4th, no infantry was available for an attack on the enemy's flank at Mount Royston. This caused the whole brunt of the fighting in this area to fall upon the cavalry, whose casualties had not been light, and whose right flank was unprotected. A squadron of the Gloucester Yeomanry from Pelusium, acting with commendable initiative, supported the right of the Australian and New Zealand cavalry from 7.45 a.m. onwards, holding off attacks from the south-east for three hours, till the composite regiment of the 5th Mounted Brigade, which had come into action at 9.45, gained touch with it. The result of the somewhat rapid advance of the Turks from the south was that General Lawrence was obliged to divert the cavalry originally destined to operate against the enemy's rear, to strengthen the line of resistance on the north. The New Zealand Mounted Rifles Brigade was directed to move from Dueidar northwards to attack the enemy's left flank, while the General Officer Commanding, 3rd Australian Light Horse Brigade, was ordered to send the regiment at Hod el Aras to Dueidar, and to bring the rest of his brigade across to Hill 70. By 12.30 p.m. the enemy on our southern flank reached the furthest point of his advance—a line running from north of Mount Royston, through Bir Abu Diyuk, along the southern slopes of Wellington Ridge, and thence bending round to the east and

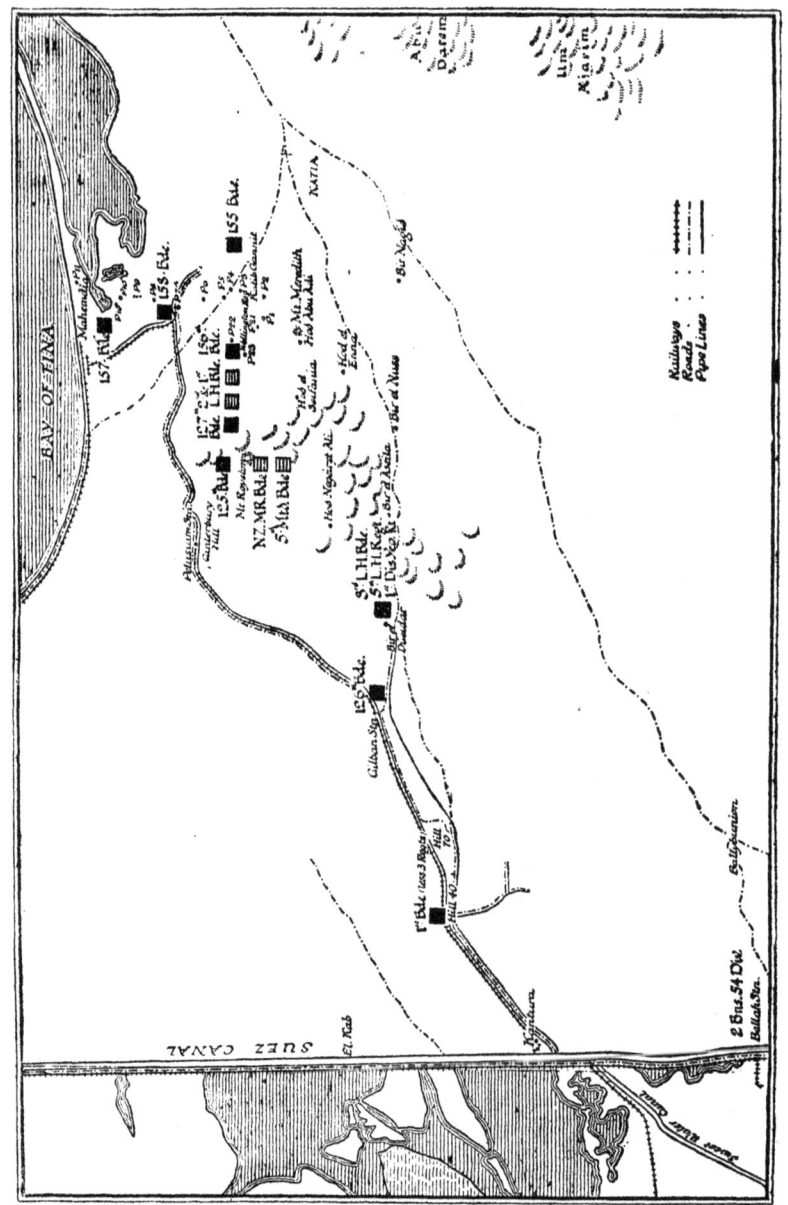

BATTLE OF ROMANI

SKETCH MAP SHOWING POSITIONS OF BRITISH TROOPS AT DUSK, 4TH AUGUST, 1916

SECOND DESPATCH

north facing the southernmost infantry post. Shortly after 1 p.m. the New Zealand Mounted Rifles Brigade with part of the 5th Mounted Brigade began to attack Mount Royston from the west. This attack was pressed slowly forward and was accompanied, in spite of heavy fire from the enemy, by a general move forward of the cavalry. By 3.30 p.m. two battalions of the 127th Brigade, closely followed by a third, were on the march southwards from Pelusium Station, and by 4 p.m. all divisions were ordered to press forward for the counter-attack, and gain and hold the line Mount Royston—Wellington Ridge. On the right, this was carried out by the Australian and New Zealand Mounted Division from the north, and the New Zealand Mounted Rifle and 5th Mounted Brigades and two battalions of the 127th Brigade from the west. By 6.30 p.m. Mount Royston, with about 500 prisoners, some machine guns and a battery of mountain artillery, was in our hands. The General Officer Commanding, 52nd Division, had already moved his reserve, consisting of the 1/5th Royal Welsh Fusiliers and 156th Brigade (less two battalions), nearer to Bir Etmaler, and by 6 p.m. the whole moved forward to attack Wellington Ridge, supported by the fire of our artillery. The ridge was strongly held, and, owing to darkness, the enemy remained in possession of part of it during the night. The result of the day's fighting was that we had repulsed a vigorous attack, capturing between 500 and 1,000 prisoners, retaken Mount Royston and part of Wellington Ridge, and were pressing back on the south a now exhausted enemy. The outpost line for the night was taken up by the leading battalions of the 42nd Division and the infantry of the 52nd Division, with some of the Australian and New Zealand cavalry in the centre. The

3rd Australian Light Horse Brigade, which had reached Hill 70, was ordered on to Dueidar, to be ready to take up the right flank of the pursuit.

Vigorous action, to the utmost limits of endurance, was ordered for the next day, and the troops, in spite of the heat, responded nobly. At daybreak, the 52nd Division, assisted by the Australian and New Zealand Mounted Division, took the remainder of Wellington Ridge by assault, capturing about 1,500 prisoners. Elsewhere the mounted troops pressed forward, meeting with some opposition, but prisoners continued to come in steadily, and it was soon obvious that the enemy's offensive was completely broken. An advance was ordered all along the line, and all mounted troops were put under the command of General Chauvel, commanding the Australian and New Zealand Mounted Division, with orders to push on as far and as vigorously as the resources at his disposal would permit.

The 42nd Division marched to Hod el Enna during the day, a very fatiguing march over extremely heavy sand. The 52nd Division met some opposition in the neighbourhood of Abu Hamra, and the high ground to the east of it was not finally occupied till late in the evening.

In the meantime the mounted troops pressed steadily forward, and found the enemy holding the ridges west of Katia, supported by artillery. The 3rd Australian Light Horse Brigade, which had moved forward from Dueidar by Bir el Nuss, came into contact with the enemy near Bir el Hamisah and captured some 450 prisoners, with machine guns and other material. The further advance of this brigade, however, was met with heavy fire from field guns and howitzers, and no further progress was made. Further northwards, as soon as the 52nd Division had cleared Abu Hamra, the advance was continued towards Katia, where the enemy's rearguard was found firmly established east of the palm trees, with both flanks well protected. A strong attempt was made to eject him by dismounted action, but the attack failed to make progress, and darkness found our troops and the enemy's facing each other, roughly on parallel lines. During the day the Royal Flying Corps reported that the retreat of the Turks was general throughout their depth, and our aeroplanes most effectively harassed his movements and threw his columns into confusion by well-directed bomb attacks.

On the morning of the 6th, the enemy was found to have retired from Katia, and, while the cavalry pressed on in pursuit, the infantry moved forward and occupied the line El Rabah—Katia—Bir el Mamluk. The 1st and 2nd Australian Light Horse Brigades, which had borne the brunt of observing and harassing the enemy's advance, were given a day's rest in camp, while the remainder of the cavalry continued the advance. The enemy's rearguard was found to be occupying his previously prepared position extending across the road and telegraph line between Hod el Reshafat and Hod el Dhakar. Our attempts to turn his flanks by Hod el Negiliat on the north and Hod el Sagia on the south were frustrated by heavy artillery fire.

On the same morning the Camel Corps detachment of Smith's Mobile Column occupied Bir el Mageibra without opposition; the 11th Australian Light Horse also moved to Mageibra, with the City of London Yeomanry in support at Bir el Jefeir. In the afternoon, Major J. J. de Knoop, Cheshire Yeomanry, commanding the Camel Corps detachment of this column, reconnoitred towards Hod el Bayud, and reported that a force of the enemy was in occupation of Hod el Muhammam, five miles north-east of Mageibra. Orders for an attack next morning were issued by Colonel Smith.

On the 7th August the cavalry maintained their action with the enemy's rearguard, which had fallen back to the line of his first entrenched position running from Oghratina to Hod el Masia, with flanks thrown well out to the north and south. There was continuous fighting throughout the day, but the enemy was too strongly supported by artillery for the cavalry to drive him from his position. Meanwhile the Mobile Column, operating from Bir el Aweidiya, had fought a very successful action with the enemy force—consisting of 1,000 rifles, three machine guns, and two 12-pounder guns—in the neighbourhood of Hod el Muhammam. The camel detachment and cavalry, the whole under the command of Lieut.-Colonel Grant, Australian Light Horse, drove the enemy out of several successive positions, capturing 53 prisoners, and successfully withdrew at nightfall. This threat to his flanks was probably an important factor in determining the enemy to continue his retreat. I regret to say that Major de Knoop, who had handled the camel detachment throughout with great skill and judgment, was killed while directing operations.

On the 8th August the enemy was found to have abandoned Oghratina, and, by the evening, to have taken up a position covering Bir el Abd, his advanced base. It was here that the enemy made his final stand to cover the evacuation of his camp and stores. Touch was now gained between the cavalry and Smith's

Mobile Column, and was maintained from this time onwards.

On the 9th August the three cavalry brigades which had hitherto carried out the pursuit were joined by a composite brigade from the 1st and 2nd Light Horse Brigades. A strong effort was made to encircle both flanks of the enemy at Bir el Abd and to cut off his further retreat. Strong opposition was, however, encountered on both flanks, and it was decided to deliver a dismounted attack with the object of driving out the enemy. Our field batteries got close enough to shell effectively the convoys removing stores from the pile at Bir el Abd, but our artillery fire drew a heavy reply from the enemy's howitzers which caused some casualties. The enemy, well supported by artillery, fought stubbornly. He made three counter-attacks, all of which were driven back with heavy loss by our rifle and machine-gun fire, and, in the evening, what appeared to be a general advance, by fresh forces, was made against our troops. This was also driven back with heavy loss, but the enemy was able to maintain his covering position. During the next two days our cavalry was unable to do more than maintain continuous pressure, but the Mobile Column, which had occupied Bayud on the 9th, continued to menace the enemy wide on his left flank. On the 10th a strong reconnaissance was made against the enemy, who was in strength at Hod el Mushalfat, south-east of Bir el Abd. On the 11th an enemy force with two mountain guns approached Bayud. A sharp action, which commenced at 5.30 a.m., was fought, and in the course of it all the baggage camels and ammunition mules of the enemy detachment were destroyed. Towards the afternoon the enemy evacuated this position, and retired on the main body of his rearguard. On the following day, patrols from the neighbourhood of Bayud found the country to the east and north all clear.

Early on the morning of the 12th it was found that the enemy had retired from Bir el Abd, and, though there was a small encounter with his rear troops about Salmana, the general pursuit stopped at this point, the enemy retiring through Bir el Mazar to El Arish. The General Officer Commanding, No. 3 Section, was ordered to hold the line Bir el Abd—Homossia with two brigades of cavalry, keeping touch with the Mobile Column which remained at Mageibra. The infantry returned to the Mahemdia—Romani line, where work on the railway was resumed with all speed. On 28th August, the 52nd Division, less the 156th Brigade, moved out to a position in the neighbourhood of El Rabah, covering the rail-head. By the end of the month most of the troops drawn from Nos. 1 and 2 Sections had returned to their sections.

7. The complete result of the operations in the Katia district was the decisive defeat and pursuit of an enemy force amounting in all to some 18,000, including 15,000 rifles. Some 4,000 prisoners, including 50 officers, were captured, and, from the number of enemy dead actually buried, it is estimated that the total number of enemy casualties amounted to about 9,000. In addition, there were captured one Krupp 75 mm. mountain battery of four guns, complete with all accessories and 400 rounds of ammunition, 9 German machine guns and mountings, with specially constructed pack saddles for camel transport, 2,300 rifles, 1,000,000 rounds small arms ammunition, 100 horses and mules, 500 camels, and a large amount of miscellaneous stores and equipment. Two field hospitals with most of their

equipment were also abandoned by the enemy in his retreat, and large quantities of stores were burnt by him at Bir el Abd to prevent their capture.

Lieut.-General the Hon. H. A. Lawrence, General Officer Commanding, No. 3 Section, directed the operations throughout, and the warmest praise is due to him and the commanders, staffs and troops concerned in the operations. General Lawrence's staff deserve great credit for their efforts in working out the allotment of camel transport, enabling our troops to conduct a vigorous pursuit. Throughout the whole month which elapsed between the enemy's first approach and his final disappearance, Major-General H. G. Chauvel, C.B., C.M.G., proved himself a resolute and resourceful cavalry leader. The brunt of the fighting fell upon the Australian and New Zealand Mounted Division, which included the Leicester, Somerset, Inverness and Ayr Batteries, R.H.A. (T.F.). I cannot speak too highly of the gallantry, steadfastness and untiring energy shown by this fine division throughout the operations. The 5th Mounted Brigade came into action successfully on 4th August, and subsequently took part in the cavalry pursuit. The 52nd Division, commanded by Major-General W. E. B. Smith, C.M.G., not only showed great steadiness under heavy artillery fire, but was responsible for the assault which recaptured Wellington Ridge on 4th August, and for clearing Abu Hamra on the 5th. Of the 42nd Division, commanded by Major-General Sir W. Douglas, K.C.M.G., C.B., only two battalions were in action on the 4th, but this division carried out a march under very trying conditions on the subsequent days. Detachments of the Bikanir Camel Corps attached to these two divisions were invaluable in reconnaissances and as escorts to small parties, besides bringing in much of the material captured.

Most excellent work was done by Lieut.-Colonel C. L. Smith, V.C., Officer Commanding, Camel Corps, and by all ranks composing the Mobile Column under his command. He executed the rôle ascribed to him with great energy and carried out his instructions with the highest intelligence. The arrangements made for mobilising and maintaining his column reflect the greatest credit on Major-General A. G. Dallas, C.B., and the staff of No. 2 Section, to which section belonged the 158th Brigade which manned part of the Romani defences on the 4th.

I cannot speak too highly of the work of the Royal Flying Corps during the whole period. Their work was extremely arduous and exhausting. The average total daily reconnaissances during the period amounted to $23\frac{1}{4}$ hours, and, during the first five days of August, to as much as $31\frac{1}{2}$ hours. Many pilots and observers were out two or three times a day for several consecutive days under very accurate anti-aircraft fire, and were frequently engaged in air combats with enemy machines of superior power. Special commendation is due to Lieut.-Colonel P. B. Joubert, Officer Commanding, 5th Wing Royal Flying Corps, and to Major H. Blackburn, Royal Flying Corps, who commanded the detachment at Kantara.

I wish also to bring to notice the good work done by H.M. Monitors M.15 and M.21, under the command of Lieut.-Commander A. O. St. John, R.N., and Commander E. Robinson, V.C., R.N., respectively. The shooting of these ships was consistently good, and they were very successful in reducing the fire of the enemy's heavy howitzers on the 4th August.

SECOND DESPATCH

8. With the exception of the operations described in the preceding paragraph, there is little to record beyond reconnaissances and patrols for the remainder of the period under review.

On 16th and 17th September, a mounted force consisting of two brigades Australian Light Horse, No. 1 Battalion Imperial Camel Corps, the Ayrshire and Inverness Batteries R.H.A., and the Hong Kong and Singapore Mountain Battery, under the command of General Officer Commanding, Australian and New Zealand Mounted Division, carried out a successful reconnaissance in force against the enemy's camp at Bir el Mazar. At dawn on the 17th the camp was attacked from the west and from the south and south-east. On the west our troops occupied a ridge about 800 yards from the enemy's second line trenches; several small posts were rushed and taken. Our batteries came into action in a favourable position, partially enfilading some enemy trenches which were seen to be occupied in strength, and inflicted considerable loss. The enemy replied actively with shell fire and heavy rifle fire. On the south and south-east our troops drew the enemy's fire on a front of two miles, and in many instances occupied the enemy's original first line trenches. My instructions were that a general action against the enemy in entrenched positions was to be avoided, and the column, having successfully carried out its mission, withdrew without any attempt on the part of the enemy to molest it. The Royal Flying Corps co-operated effectively throughout the operation, and the gallant action of the seaplanes of the Royal Naval Air Service off El Arish diverted the attention of the enemy's aircraft from our troops at Bir el Mazar. Our casualties were slight, and our captures included one officer and 13 men of the enemy's camel corps, besides a number of camels.

The success of this operation, apart from the casualties inflicted, which were heavy, lay in the fact that it gave the enemy a new and unexpected proof of our extended radius of action, and induced him, in the course of the next few days, to evacuate his camp at Bir el Mazar and withdraw the troops to camps near El Arish.

On 18th September, Major-General Sir Charles Dobell, K.C.B., C.M.G., D.S.O., took over temporary command of No. 3 Section.

In No. 1 Section during the month of September, various small reconnaissances were made. The most important of these was carried out against Bir el Tawal (about 30 miles west of El Kubri) by a column under Brigadier-General A. Mudge, between the 14th and 21st September. The column included half a squadron Middlesex Yeomanry, one troop Hertfordshire Yeomanry, two companies 1/5th Bedfordshire Regiment, and one company each of the 1/4th Northamptonshire and 1/10th London Regiments. The approach march was excellently carried out over very broken and intricate country. The enemy's position was reached on the 17th, and, after a preliminary reconnaissance on that day, an attack was made early the next morning. The infantry advanced with great dash, and almost immediately the enemy took to flight, but pursuit was impossible owing to the nature of the ground. An inspection of the enemy's camp showed that he had been completely taken by surprise, and had left behind all his stores and personal effects, which were captured. After the wells had been emptied, and such stores as could not be brought away had been destroyed, our troops withdrew, reaching Kubri rail-head on 21st September. Our total casualties were three other ranks killed and two other ranks wounded.

On the western front during the months of August and September there has been little of note to report. The railway towards the Baharia oasis has been pushed on, and the rail-head of the Kharga railway is now 10 miles beyond Kharga Station. Patrolling has been most active in all sections of the line. On 31st August a patrol of eight motor-cars captured an enemy camel convoy 20 miles north-west of Jarabub. The escort of 30 armed men surrendered without resistance, the loads and saddles of the camels were burnt and most of the camels destroyed. In the Baharia section a patrol of two officers and three men, Imperial Camel Corps, came in contact with a small body of between 15 and 20 enemy near the point where the " Rubi " road from Samalut descends the escarpment of the Baharia oasis. The two officers became detached from the men, who made their way back to the post covering the rail-head, but I much regret that subsequent search has failed to discover the missing officers. In the Wadi Natron section a motor-car patrol on 21st September arrested a small convoy under a Tripolitan officer of the Senoussi Force, which was bringing mails and a quantity of bombs, gelignite and automatic pistols from Baharia to Amria (12 miles west of Alexandria on the coast).

On the 18th September, Brigadier-General E. A. Herbert, M.V.O., was appointed to temporary command of the Western Frontier Force.

Throughout the period under review the command of the Delta district and the Lines of Communication Defences has been held by Major-General W. A. Watson, C.B., C.I.E., and the duties of that command, though happily involving no active operations, have been carried out to my satisfaction. Great activity and thoroughness has been shown in carrying out my instructions to establish a line of posts along the western edge of the Canal Zone, to prevent the entrance of undesirable persons. The patrolling duties involved have been entrusted to two squadrons of the 4th Australian Light Horse Regiment, who have displayed the greatest zeal, tact and resource in bringing the new orders and restrictions into force. The results of this measure have been excellent, and the Western Canal Zone can now be said to be free from the presence of all unauthorised persons.

9. It gives me the greatest pleasure to bring to notice the services rendered by General Sir F. R. Wingate, G.C.B., G.C.V.O., K.C.M.G., D.S.O., and the Egyptian Army since the beginning of the war to the Mediterranean Expeditionary Force and the Egyptian Expeditionary Force, and to express my gratefulness for the assistance which has at all times been so willingly given. Fifty-eight officers and 12 Sudan Government officials served—most of them for short periods equivalent to the amount of leave to which, in normal circumstances, they would have been entitled—with the Mediterranean Expeditionary Force; of these, six officers were either killed or died of wounds, 11 were wounded. Sixty officers and 27 Sudan Government officials were lent at various times for service with the Egyptian Expeditionary Force.

Personnel of the Egyptian Army has been employed at different times as guards for railway bridges and to garrison various important points in the interior. The Egyptian Army also supplied guns and gunners for two armoured trains for use with the defences of Egypt.

SECOND DESPATCH

A Camel Maxim Section and an armed detachment of the Military Works Department were attached to the Bikanir Camel Corps, and took part in the operations against the Senoussi (in which operations No. 1 Squadron Egyptian Cavalry was also employed) and in the attack on the Suez Canal in April, 1915. Two companies of the 2nd (Egyptian) Battalion garrisoned Tor in January, 1915, and took part in the subsequent operations in that district. The garrison of Abu Zeneima was also supplied for some months by troops of the Egyptian Army. In the course of 1915, 2,230 Egyptian reservists, who had been called up, were employed on works connected with the Canal defences; a number of Egyptian officers, from pension and unemployed lists, volunteered for service with these reservists and gave valuable assistance. A works battalion of six companies was formed in May, 1915, for service at the Dardanelles, the battalion and the companies being commanded by British officers in the employ of the Egyptian Army. This unit did excellent work, under perpetual shell fire, on the Peninsula, during the four months of its employment.

Besides this assistance in the matter of personnel, the Egyptian Army has most liberally placed at the disposal of the Mediterranean and Egyptian Expeditionary Forces accommodation, war material and transport camels.

I would especially mention the loan of the Egyptian Army Hospital at Cairo, complete with equipment, to the New Zealand Division; the purchase in the Sudan of over 14,000 riding and baggage camels, the collection, veterinary examination and despatch of which threw a large amount of additional work upon the province staffs; the supply of 174,000 grenades for the Mediterranean Expeditionary Force; the loan of tugs and steel plates for the Canal defences; and the manufacture and repair, in the Stores Department, of a large number of articles of equipment and clothing. For these, and all other, services rendered in addition to their normal duties, the Egyptian Army and the Sudan Administration deserve the most cordial thanks.

I also wish to express my extreme gratefulness to Field Marshal the Rt. Hon. Lord Methuen, G.C.B., G.C.V.O., C.M.G., Governor and Commander-in-Chief, Malta, and to all his staff, for the labours which they have undertaken in connection with hospital work for the benefit of the Mediterranean and Egyptian Expeditionary Forces. In March and April, 1915, the accommodation in Malta for sick and wounded began to expand, and rose from 321 beds in February to 22,000 beds at the end of 1915. The additional accommodation required was found by the construction of new hospitals in existing barracks, schools, and other buildings, and by the erection of tented hospitals and convalescent camps. During the operations on the Gallipoli Peninsula and up to the evacuation of Mudros, 2,361 officers and 57,293 men were admitted from transports and hospital ships. During March, 1916, this accommodation was reduced to 12,000 beds with a corresponding reduction in personnel, but, since July, expansion to meet the demands of the Salonica Force has steadily proceeded, till, at the end of August, there were 21,174 beds on the Island, with the possibility of expansion up to 27,000. By the beginning of September a total of 854 officers and 23,119 men had been received from the Salonica Force.

The expansion, reduction, and re-expansion of accommodation has necessitated very hard work on the

SECOND DESPATCH

part of the Engineer, Barracks, Ordnance, Transport and Supply Services, as well as on the part of the Medical Department.

I wish to call attention to the admirable work that has been performed by the Nursing Services in the hospitals in Egypt. Not only have they had to deal with a very large number of wounded and sick from Gallipoli, Salonica and Egypt itself, but also from other theatres of war. The devotion to duty, zeal and skill of the Nursing Services, British, Australian and New Zealand, and of the voluntary helpers, have been beyond praise, and I shall have great pleasure in bringing to your notice in a subsequent despatch the names of a number of these ladies for specially distinguished service.

The distribution by the Army Postal Service of letters and parcels over the extended desert fronts has been fraught with difficulties. The successful manner in which these have been overcome has greatly contributed to the comfort and health of the troops under my command. In this connection I wish to acknowledge the assistance I have received from the Egyptian Postal Service, under the able direction of N. T. Borton Pasha, Postmaster-General.

The complete failure of the enemy's operations in August was largely due to the manner in which the plans for defence were prepared, and the distribution of the troops arranged. In the accomplishment of this, the Chief of my General Staff, Major-General A. L. Lynden-Bell, C.B., C.M.G., rendered me able and devoted service. His work has been of an onerous nature, and he has discharged it with energy, skill and determination.

My thanks are also due to Lieut.-General E. A.

Altham, K.C.B., C.M.G., for the manner in which he has discharged his responsible duties as Inspector-General of Communications.

I will submit in a separate despatch the names of those officers and men who have rendered distinguished service during the period under review, and whose services I desire to commend.

    I have the honour to be, Sir,
        Your most obedient Servant,
            (Signed) A. J. MURRAY, General,
                  Commander-in-Chief,
                  Egyptian Expeditionary Force.

COVERING LETTER SENT WITH SECOND DESPATCH
11th October, 1916

COVERING LETTER SENT WITH SECOND DESPATCH

From—
    THE COMMANDER-IN-CHIEF,
        Egyptian Expeditionary Force.

To—
    THE SECRETARY OF STATE FOR WAR,
        War Office, London, S.W.

General Headquarters,
Egyptian Expeditionary Force,
11th October, 1916.

SIR,

I have the honour to forward herewith my despatch dealing with operations between 1st June and 30th September.

I am aware that, as in my last despatch, there are certain passages which it will not be advisable to publish at present. I wish, therefore, in order to avoid delay in publication, to express my willingness that such passages should be deleted by the General Staff without any further reference to me, while respectfully requesting that the general sequence and connection of the whole should be preserved.

    I have the honour to be, Sir,
      Your most obedient Servant,
        (Signed) A. J. MURRAY, General,
          Commander-in-Chief,
          Egyptian Expeditionary Force.

THIRD DESPATCH

1st March, 1917

LIEUTENANT-GENERAL SIR H. G. CHAUVEL, K.C.M.G., C.B.

THIRD DESPATCH

From—
    THE COMMANDER-IN-CHIEF,
        Egyptian Expeditionary Force.

To—
    THE SECRETARY OF STATE FOR WAR,
        War Office, London, S.W.

General Headquarters,
Egyptian Expeditionary Force,
1st March, 1917.

MY LORD,

I have the honour to submit a report on the operations of the Force under my command from 1st October, 1916, to 28th February, 1917.

1. During the months of October and November and the first half of December, there were no important operations upon my eastern front, though a successful reconnaissance against the enemy positions at El Rakwa and Bir el Maghara, 65 miles east of Ismailia, was carried out between the 13th and 17th October by a small force of Australian Light Horse, Yeomanry and Camel Corps. This operation not only needed careful preparation, but entailed two night marches over exceedingly difficult sand-dune country, the difficulties being increased on the second night by the presence of a thick fog. On the early morning of the 15th, the enemy was located holding a strong position on the high precipitous hills of Maghara. The force, attacking in two columns, dislodged the enemy from his advanced position, capturing a few prisoners. At the same time

the enemy's camp was repeatedly bombed by our aeroplanes, which furnished invaluable assistance throughout the operation. After an engagement lasting two hours, the force withdrew unmolested, and reached Bayud on the 17th without the loss of a single camel. The operation was well carried out, and valuable information was obtained regarding the enemy's dispositions and the nature of the country.

With this exception, all was quiet on the eastern front. The unexpected evidence of our mobility given to the enemy by the successful reconnaissance against Bir el Mazar which I recorded in my last despatch, and the losses suffered by the Turks during this affair, had given the enemy sufficient uneasiness to induce him to withdraw altogether from Mazar, and towards the end of October his nearest troops were in the neighbourhood of Ujret el Zol and Masaid, about seven and four miles west of El Arish respectively. The enemy also maintained several small posts in the neighbourhood of Maghara, with small garrisons further south at Hassana and Nekhl. About the same time the railway towards El Arish, which had been making steady and uninterrupted progress, was in the neighbourhood of Bir Salmana, some four miles east of Bir el Abd. The Australian and New Zealand Mounted Division, with the 5th Mounted Brigade attached, had advanced from Romani, and was covering the advance and the railway construction east of Salmana with brigades thrown out to its flanks and rear; the 52nd Division was at Bir el Abd, and the 42nd Division disposed along the line of communication from Kantara to Negiliat (half-way between Romani and Bir el Abd).

2. On the 23rd October, in order to be in closer touch with the civil authority, I moved my General

THIRD DESPATCH

Headquarters from Ismailia to Cairo, and at the same time the new Headquarters of the Eastern Force came into existence at Ismailia, under the command of Lieut.-General Sir Charles Dobell, K.C.B., C.M.G., D.S.O. This new command included the three sections of the Canal Defences, of which I have previously spoken, and the Sharqia province (between the edge of the Nile Delta and the Suez Canal), including Port Said and Suez. At the same time the Headquarters of the Inspector-General of Communications, which had always been in Cairo, were merged in General Headquarters, and, on the lapse of his appointment, Lieut.-General Sir E. A. Altham, K.C.B., C.M.G., to my great personal regret, returned to England. During the first half of November further modifications were made in the organisation of the force under my command, and I made a general redistribution of troops in the Eastern Force so as to set free a sufficient force for mobile operations during the next stages of the advance. Arrangements were completed for the abolition of the three sections of the Canal Defences; for the amalgamation of the old Nos. 1 and 2 Sections into the Southern Canal Section; and for the division of the old No. 3 Section into two parts—one being the Desert Column, which, for the time being, was composed of the Australian and New Zealand Mounted Division and the 42nd and 52nd Divisions, and the other being called the Northern Canal Section and practically forming the lines of communication of the Desert Column. The Northern Canal Section at first extended from the Canal as far east as Romani, and will soon extend to El Arish. I also made preparation for a considerable reduction of the garrison in the Southern Canal Section, and for the withdrawal of the 53rd Division altogether from this area to form the general reserve of the Eastern Force. All these preparations were completed during the first half of November, and took effect between the 22nd November and 5th December, by which time the whole of the 42nd Division had been relieved from its line of communication duties and concentrated at Mazar. The 53rd Division was concentrated in reserve at Ismailia and El Ferdan, while the Desert Column and the Northern and Southern Canal Sections were formed as above described.

3. The first half of November was mainly occupied in making the necessary arrangements for pressing forward our advance towards El Arish. In the south a small column under Brigadier-General P. C. Palin, C.B., marched on Bir um Gurf, 30 miles south-east of Suez, on the 15th and 16th November, and attacked and drove off some enemy posted in the hills. On the north, construction was begun of a strong defensive position which I had ordered to be made covering Bir el Abd; this position has since been prepared for defence with the greatest possible completeness.

During the latter part of the month the Australian and New Zealand Mounted Division gradually pushed forward in advance of the railway, which by November 26th reached Mazar. Reconnaissances by mounted troops were pushed forward to within eight miles of El Arish by 17th November, when the enemy's outposts were located at Ujret el Zol; on November 28th a mounted patrol was pushed through to Bir el Masmi, little more than three miles south-west of El Arish; and from this time our patrols were constantly in touch with the enemy's position at El Arish—Masaid. Throughout the month the enemy's aircraft showed considerable activity, attacking the rail-head and bivouacs of our advanced troops with bombs. Little damage, however, was done, and our own aircraft retained complete superiority in the air. The Royal Flying Corps in this month visited El Magdhaba (see Map 3), Sheikh Zowaid, and Khan Yunus, for reconnaissance purposes, and on the 11th November made very successful bomb attacks on Beersheba and El Magdhaba. At Beersheba special attention was paid to the aerodrome and the railway station, both of which were extensively damaged. Presumably in retaliation for the air raid at Beersheba, one hostile aeroplane dropped bombs on Cairo on the 13th, causing some casualties among the civil population and killing one private; no other damage of a military nature was done. The Royal Flying Corps promptly replied by heavily bombing the enemy's camp at El Magdhaba by moonlight on the same night. On the 17th November the enemy's camps at Masaid were heavily bombed by four machines in reply to the appearance of a hostile machine at Suez the same morning.

By the 1st December the railway had reached Kilometre 121, about five miles east of Mazar. At this time the Australian and New Zealand Mounted Division, supported by part of the 42nd Division, was in advance of and covering the rail-head; the remainder of the 42nd Division was at Mazar. The 52nd Division, less one brigade, reached Mazar on the 2nd December; the 53rd Division (general reserve), less one infantry brigade and attached troops, was moving up to Romani. During the first week of December constant patrols were sent out by the Australian and New Zealand Mounted Division, and the country was thoroughly reconnoitred in the area Mazar—Risan Aneiza—Bir Lahfan (see Map 4) —Bir el Masmi. In the meantime, the enemy maintained his position of El Arish and Masaid, and, in order to afford him no inducement to withdraw until such time as I should be ready to strike, mounted patrols were ordered to be as unostentatious as possible.

4. On the 7th December Lieut.-General Sir P. W. Chetwode, Bt., C.B., D.S.O., assumed command of the Desert Column, shortly afterwards moving his Headquarters from Bir el Abd to Mazar. By the 10th the railway was within 20 miles of El Arish, and the time had come which was to reward the strenuous labours of nearly a year. Since January, the force had gradually pushed right across the Sinai desert, fighting when necessary, organising and constructing incessantly in the heavy sand and hot sun. The pressure on the enemy in other theatres, and our success at Romani, were undoubtedly contributing factors to this advance, but the main factor—without which all liberty of action and any tactical victory would have been nugatory— —was work, intense and unremitting. To regain this peninsula, the true frontier of Egypt, hundreds of miles of road and railway had been built,[1] hundreds of miles of water-piping had been laid, filters capable of supplying 1,500,000 gallons of water a day, and reservoirs with a total capacity of 3,500,000 gallons had been installed, and 900,000 tons of stone transported from distant quarries. Kantara had been transformed from a small canal village into an important railway and water terminus, with wharves and cranes and a railway ferry; and the desert, till then almost destitute of human habitation, showed the successive marks of our advance in the shape of strong positions firmly entrenched and protected by hundreds of miles of barbed wire, of standing camps where troops could shelter in

[1] The figures up to the end of February are as follows :—388 miles of railway, 203 miles of metalled road, 86 miles of wire and brushwood road, 300 miles of water-piping; 960,000 tons of stone quarried.

THIRD DESPATCH

comfortable huts, of tanks and reservoirs built of concrete, of railway stations and sidings, of aerodromes and of signal stations and wireless installations, by all of which the desert was subdued and made habitable, and adequate lines of communication established between the advancing troops and their ever-receding base. Moreover, not only had British troops laboured incessantly through the summer and autumn, but the body of organised native labour had grown till the Egyptian Labour Corps, with its special headquarters, standing camps, clearing camps and recruiting stations, had reached a total of nearly 40,000.[1] The necessity of combining the protection and maintenance, including the important work of sanitation, of this large force of workers, British and native, with that steady progress on the railway, roads and pipes which was vital to the success of my operations, put the severest strain upon all energies and resources; but the problem of feeding the workers without starving the work was solved by the good-will and energy of all concerned, and it was only the period of active operations in August, and one or two delays in the arrival of material by sea, that stopped the steady eastward movement of pipes and lines.

Moreover, organisation kept pace with construction. The equipment of the fighting units with camel transport, which had reached its first stage of completion at the time of the Romani battle, had been perfected by the middle of December. The three divisions of the Desert Column were provided with some 3,000 camels each, and a proportionate number of native drivers, furnishing complete first-line transport, which had been worked out in the minutest detail, for each of their

[1] This number is now 50,000, and is still increasing.

component units. A large number of additional camels were provided for convoying supplies and water from the rail-head to the front. The haulage of artillery had been lightened by the fitting of ped-rails, and all surplus horses—the watering of which was a serious burden—were withdrawn. The striking force was now completely mobile, and the troops had grown skilful in meeting the special problems of desert campaigning.

5. But no organisation could entirely overcome the chief difficulty which had faced us all through the year, the adequate provision of water for the troops. In fact, during this final period this difficulty was accentuated by the rapid advance of troops and railway, with which the water-supply could not keep pace. Moreover, my troops had passed out of the water-bearing Katia basin, and had reached a tract in which local water was almost non-existent. From Romani to Bir el Abd the local water, though generally somewhat brackish, had been always employed for the horses, mules and camels, and it had been found that, if the necessary precautions were taken, it had no ill-effect upon our troops, at all events for a limited period. East of Bir el Abd the situation is altogether different. Water is found in comparatively few and widely-separated localities. Such as exists is generally too brackish for human consumption, and the wells east of the water-line are so widely separated and are of so small capacity that it is a matter of great difficulty—sometimes a complete impossibility—to water any large number of animals. This latter fact greatly restricted the employment of mounted troops. During the first half of November, also, the 12-inch pipe-line was not yet delivering water at Romani, and the water for the advanced troops had therefore to be brought up by rail in tank trucks, and stored in im-

provised tanks at railway-sidings made for that purpose. Since the railway had reached Kilometre 109 by 14th November, considerable strain was thrown on its resources for this period, owing to the necessity for maintaining the rate of construction, for forwarding material for the construction of the 12-inch pipe-line, for supplying the troops, and for undertaking the long haulage of great quantities of water in addition. By the 17th November, however, the water situation was somewhat relieved by the delivery of water through the 12-inch pipe-line at Romani. This reduced by 25 miles the distance over which water had to be hauled by the railway. Thereafter the water difficulty again increased as the railway advanced, until on the 1st December the 12-inch pipe-line delivered water at Bir el Abd, thereby again reducing the distance over which rail-borne water had to be carried. But as the month advanced, the water question presented itself more insistently than ever as the one factor which would determine the day when I could strike at El Arish. Every tactical preparation for the offensive had been made, naval co-operation planned, and arrangements made for the landing of stores and construction of piers as soon as the place was in my possession. But the difficulty of water-supply, even with rail-head only 15 miles to the rear, was immense. The enemy was so disposed as to cover all the available water in the neighbourhood of El Arish and Masaid. Between his position and ours, and south of his position, no water could be found; nor had search in the Wadi el Arish, south of the town, by parties sent in by night, proved more successful. The enemy was disposed in depth covering all the water in the area—there being about four miles between his outpost line and his third line of defence. If, therefore, he should be able to force us to spend two days in the operation of driving him from his position, it would be necessary to carry forward very large quantities of water on camels for the men and animals of the formations engaged. This entailed the establishment of a very large reserve of water at rail-head, and the preparation of elaborate arrangements for the forwarding and distribution of water.

The size of the Turkish garrison at El Arish was known to me with approximate certainty. It consisted of two battalions of the 80th Regiment of the 3rd Turkish Division—some 1,600 infantry in all—in a strong entrenched position. Between the 9th and 14th December, increased activity was shown by the Turks, and our aircraft and mounted patrols reported the construction of new works, while the enemy camps at Magdhaba and Abu Aweigila were reported to have increased in size. On these indications of a probable reinforcement to the enemy, the final preparations were pushed on with most strenuous determination. Had rain only fallen, an earlier move could have been made, but as it was, the water-supply for the striking force of two infantry divisions, the Australian and New Zealand Mounted Division, and the Imperial Camel Corps Brigade, was not adequately secured till 20th December.

6. The swiftness of our final preparations was rewarded, but not immediately, by a successful engagement. We had been too quick for the enemy, but he had recognised it, and, knowing that reinforcements would arrive too late, had hurriedly withdrawn his troops from Masaid and El Arish. This retirement was reported by the Royal Flying Corps on the 20th December, and the Australian and New Zealand

THIRD DESPATCH 99

Mounted Division and Imperial Camel Corps Brigade were ordered to move on El Arish the same night. The 52nd Division was to move in support of the mounted troops. Accordingly, after a skilfully conducted march of 20 miles in the moonless night, the 1st and 3rd Light Horse Brigades and the Imperial Camel Corps Brigade surrounded the enemy's position. Light Horse patrols reached El Arish about sunrise, and found it unoccupied. By 7.20 a.m. the 1st Light Horse Brigade was east of El Arish, the Imperial Camel Corps south of the town, the 3rd Light Horse Brigade was about Masaid, and the New Zealand Mounted Rifles Brigade was at Masmi. Subsequently, the General Officer Commanding, Desert Column, reported that there was no necessity for naval co-operation, since the enemy had completely evacuated his position. Owing to the fact that insufficient water had been found, the 42nd Division was sent back to Mazar. During the day our aircraft reported about 1,600 of the enemy on the march in two columns in the neighbourhood of Magdhaba and Abu Aweigila. Sheikh Zowaid and Rafa appeared to be clear of the enemy. Maghara had been evacuated, and the enemy was apparently in process of withdrawing from the neighbouring posts. By the night of the 21st December, therefore, the reoccupation of El Arish had been effected, and the enemy was evacuating, or had evacuated, his positions west of a north and south line through that place, except those at Nekhl and Hassana. The aircraft, moreover, reported that the garrison of the latter place seemed also to be reduced.

On the 22nd December the 52nd Division was about El Arish and El Bittia. Mine-sweeping operations were at once commenced in the roadstead, under the direction of Captain A. H. Williamson, M.V.O., R.N., while the erection of a pier was taken in hand by the Royal Australian Naval Bridging Train. In 48 hours the roadstead was cleared of mines, and the supply ships from Port Said began unloading stores and supplies on the 24th. Supplies were also hastened to El Arish by camel convoy, since it was of the utmost importance to accumulate at once a sufficient amount to give our mounted troops a further radius of action. Our aircraft were exceedingly active during the day. A successful attack was made on the railway bridge at Tel el Sharia, north of Beersheba; El Auja and Beersheba were effectively bombed; and two battalions of Turkish troops located by the Royal Flying Corps at Magdhaba, some 20 miles south of El Arish, were attacked with bombs by 13 of our aeroplanes, and suffered many casualties.

In order to emphasise the capture of El Arish, in the Southern Canal Section a column assembled near Bir Mabeiuk on the 22nd December, and on the following days advanced through the Mitla Pass and by the Darb el Haj as far as Sudr el Heitan, more than half-way to Nekhl. This column destroyed various enemy posts and entrenchments, but, finding no enemy, returned on the 25th.

7. The enemy having temporarily succeeded in eluding us, it was of the utmost importance to strike any of his forces that remained within our reach. I had always anticipated that, should the enemy choose to abandon El Arish, his line of retreat would be through Magdhaba and Abu Aweigila towards El Auja. These anticipations were confirmed by the report of the Royal Flying Corps that an enemy force of about two regiments was at Magdhaba. It appeared likely that this

MAJOR-GENERAL CHAUVEL AND STAFF OF THE ANZAC MOUNTED DIVISION

force consisted of the 1,600 infantry which had composed the garrison of El Arish, and that it was preparing to hold Magdhaba as a rearguard. Orders were given that a mounted force should push forward with all haste against the enemy, and arrangements were made accordingly by General Sir Charles Dobell for the move of the Australian and New Zealand Mounted Division, less the 2nd Light Horse Brigade, with the Imperial Camel Brigade, against Magdhaba and Abu Aweigila on the night of the 22nd/23rd. Major-General Sir H. G. Chauvel, K.C.M.G., C.B., was in command of the column.

8. Starting at 12.45 a.m. on December 23rd, the Flying Column halted at 4.50 a.m. in an open plain about four miles from Magdhaba, whence the enemy's bivouac fires could plainly be seen. General Chauvel with his Staff and subordinate commanders immediately undertook a personal reconnaissance of the enemy's position, and soon after 8 a.m., by which time the first aeroplane reports had been received, the attack was set in motion.

The enemy had taken up a position on both banks of the Wadi el Arish, and was very strongly posted in a rough circle of from 3,000 to 3,500 yards diameter. Five large closed works, exceedingly well-sited, formed the principal defences, and between these works was a system of well-constructed and concealed trenches and rifle pits. General Chauvel's plan of attack was as follows :

The New Zealand Mounted Rifles Brigade and the 3rd Light Horse Brigade, both under the command of Brigadier-General E. W. C. Chaytor, C.B., were to move to the east of Magdhaba and to swing round to attack the enemy's right and rear. The Imperial Camel

Corps Brigade was to move direct against Magdhaba to attack the enemy in front—that is, from the north-west. The 1st Light Horse Brigade was at the outset in reserve. Between 8.45 a.m. and 9.30 a.m. the attack developed, and at the latter hour General Chaytor moved a light horse regiment and part of a machine-gun squadron on a wide turning movement round the rear of the enemy's position, with orders to come in from the south. A little later, two regiments of the New Zealand Mounted Rifles Brigade were despatched in more or less the same direction, though making a less wide detour, with orders to move on Magdhaba from the east. In the meantime the Imperial Camel Corps Brigade was making progress, though somewhat slowly.

At 10 a.m. the aircraft reports indicated the possibility that the enemy might try to escape. Thereupon General Chauvel ordered the 1st Light Horse Brigade, less one regiment remaining in reserve, to push in from the north-west. The brigade moved forward at a trot, and, coming under shrapnel fire, increased the pace to a gallop. The enemy then opened a very heavy rifle and machine-gun fire, whereupon the brigade swung to its right and gained cover in the Wadi, where, dismounting, it began an attack against the left of the enemy position.

Between noon and 1.30 p.m. the enemy's position was practically surrounded, but for some little time it had been found increasingly difficult to make progress. The horse-artillery batteries had been greatly hindered by the mirage and the difficulty of getting forward observation, the ground round the enemy's position being absolutely flat and devoid of cover. The Hong Kong and Singapore Camel Battery was in action at less than 2,000 yards range.

THIRD DESPATCH

In the meantime reports were received from the Field Squadron that no water could be found. Unless Magdhaba could be taken during the day, therefore, it was probable that our troops would have to withdraw, as none of the horses had been watered since the evening of the 22nd, and the nearest water, except that in the enemy's position, was at El Arish. General Chauvel reported the situation to the Desert Column accordingly, and received orders to maintain the attack at all hazards.

But even before this communication arrived, the situation had begun to improve. The 1st Light Horse Brigade, pressing on against the enemy's left, captured a work on the west of the Wadi, taking about 100 prisoners. At 2 p.m. two regiments of the 3rd Light Horse Brigade, coming in from the north-east, were within 200 yards of the position, in close touch with the Imperial Camel Corps Brigade advancing from the north-west. A quarter of an hour later the attack of the remaining regiment of this brigade was pressing heavily on the enemy from the south. By three o'clock the New Zealand Mounted Rifles Brigade was within 600 yards of the enemy's trenches on the east.

From this time forward the pressure on the enemy increased on all sides. Before 3.30 p.m. the 1st Light Horse Brigade and the Imperial Camel Corps Brigade attacked the second line of the enemy's trenches, and at 4 p.m. the former brigade carried one of the main redoubts, taking 130 prisoners, including the Turkish commander. Immediately after this, part of the 10th Light Horse Regiment charged in from the south, mounted and with fixed bayonets, and by 4.30 p.m. all organised resistance was over, and the enemy was surrendering everywhere.

The total number of prisoners taken in this fine action was 1,282, including some 50 wounded. A large number of the enemy were buried by our troops on the position. Four mountain guns, one machine gun and 1,052 rifles were captured, and 200 more rifles were destroyed.

Our own casualties were 12 officers and 134 other ranks killed and wounded. It was possible to give every attention to our wounded before moving them back to El Arish, owing to the fact that the enemy had a permanent and well-equipped hospital at Magdhaba, to which they were taken as soon as the action was over.

The troops marched back to El Arish during the night of December 23rd/24th.

9. On the 27th December the Royal Flying Corps reported that an entrenched position was being prepared by the enemy at El Magruntein, near Rafa. Work on this position was continued during the following day, and it was occupied by a garrison equivalent to about two battalions, with mountain guns. Since the railway was only just reaching El Arish, where extensive work on the station and sidings would be necessary, it was not at the moment possible for me, owing to difficulties of supply, to push on and occupy Rafa permanently. Since, however, the enemy had again placed a small detached garrison within striking distance of my mounted troops, I determined, if possible, to repeat the success at Magdhaba, by surrounding and capturing the Magruntein position also. I communicated this decision on 7th January to General Dobell, who entrusted the operation to Lieut.-General Sir Philip Chetwode, Bt., C.B., D.S.O., commanding the Desert Column, who set out from El Arish on the evening of

the 8th/9th with a force consisting of the Australian and New Zealand Mounted Division (less one brigade), the 5th Mounted Brigade and the Imperial Camel Corps Brigade, with the Hong Kong and Singapore Battery attached.

So efficiently and swiftly was the approach-march carried out that the enemy was completely surprised, and by dawn on 9th January his position was almost entirely surrounded before he became aware of the presence of any large forces in his vicinity. The position, however, was a formidable one. It consisted of three strong series of works connected by trenches, one series facing west, one facing south-west, and one facing south and south-east. The whole was dominated by a central keep or redoubt, some 2,000 yards south-west of Rafa. Moreover, the ground in front of these works was entirely open and devoid of cover, and, in their immediate neighbourhood, was almost a glacis.

The guns, with which aeroplanes were co-operating, started to register at 7.20 a.m. The main attack, to be carried out by Major-General Sir H. G. Chauvel, K.C.M.G., C.B., General Officer Commanding, Australian and New Zealand Mounted Division, was timed for 10 a.m., with the New Zealand Mounted Rifles Brigade on the right, attacking from the east, and the 1st Light Horse Brigade on their left, attacking from the east and south-east, while the Imperial Camel Corps attacked the works in their front from the south-east. The 3rd Light Horse Brigade was in reserve, and the 5th Mounted Brigade in column reserve. Shortly after 10 a.m. parties of Turks, who were attempting to leave Rafa by the Khan Yunus road, were met and captured by the New Zealand Brigade, who galloped the Police Barracks and a machine-gun post, capturing six

Germans (including one officer), two Turkish officers, and 163 other ranks.

Before 11 a.m. Rafa was occupied, and two regiments of the 3rd Light Horse Brigade were advanced against the works on the left of the 1st Light Horse Brigade. The 1st Light Horse Brigade with the Camel Brigade was ordered to press its attack on the works facing south-west, and about the same time the remainder of the New Zealand Brigade, with the 1st Light Horse Brigade, galloped an open space south of the Police post, and established itself 300 yards east of the nearest enemy work. The 5th Mounted Brigade was also ordered to deploy against the western works and to attack in conjunction with the Camel Brigade. The encircling movement was now practically complete, save for a gap in the north-west between the New Zealand Brigade and the Yeomanry. At 12.20 p.m. "B" Battery, Honourable Artillery Company, moved forward some 1,500 yards to support the attack of the 5th Mounted Brigade. By 1 p.m. our troops were within 600 yards of the southern and western trenches, which were being shelled with good effect by our artillery. By 2 p.m. the right of the New Zealand Mounted Rifles Brigade had linked up with the left of the 5th Mounted Brigade, and was pressing its attack on the rear of one of the enemy works. General Chetwode now issued orders for a concerted attack on the "Redoubt," or central keep, by the New Zealand Brigade and all other available troops of the Australian and New Zealand Mounted Division, to commence at 3.30 p.m. The 5th Mounted Brigade was ordered to co-operate against the rear of the work. By 3.15 two of the enemy's works had been captured, and further prisoners had been taken.

THIRD DESPATCH

While the attack on the central redoubt was developing, information was received, both from patrols and from the Royal Flying Corps, that an enemy relieving force, estimated at 1,500 men, was marching from Shellal on Rafa. This force was attacked frequently with bombs and machine-gun fire by our aeroplanes with success. General Chetwode did not allow this threat, which complicated his situation, to affect the execution of his purpose. He at once gave orders for the attack to be pressed with vigour, and issued instructions that, if the position were not captured by 5 p.m., the engagement was to be broken off, and the force to be withdrawn under cover of darkness. The troops, admirably supported by the artillery, advanced with great gallantry, and at 4.45 p.m. the New Zealand Brigade captured the redoubt with brilliant dash, covering the last 800 yards in two rushes supported by machine-gun fire. By this achievement they were able to take the lower-lying works in reverse, and these soon fell to the Camel Brigade, the Yeomanry and the Australian Light Horse. By 5.30 p.m. all organised resistance was over, and the enemy's position with all its garrison was captured, while the 3rd Light Horse Brigade, which had come in contact with the detachment marching from Shellal, drove off the enemy without difficulty. The force now withdrew, taking with them all prisoners, animals and material captured; one regiment and a light car patrol, which were left to clear the battlefield, withdrew unmolested on the following day.

In this fine action, which lasted for 10 hours, the entire enemy force, with its commander, was accounted for. More than 1,600 unwounded prisoners were taken, including one German officer and five German non-commissioned officers. In addition, six machine guns, four mountain guns and a number of camels and mules were captured. Our casualties were comparatively light, amounting to 487 in all, of which 71 were killed, 415 wounded, and one was missing.

10. The result of these successful operations was that the province of Sinai, which for two years had been partially occupied by the Turks, was freed of all formed bodies of Turkish troops. The destruction of his rearguard at Magdhaba compelled the enemy to withdraw from Maghara, Hassana and Nekhl, all of which were clear by the 31st December, and the victory at Magruntein had driven him over the frontier at Rafa, which he did not attempt to reoccupy. For this achievement I am greatly indebted to Lieut.-General Sir Charles Dobell, K.C.B., C.M.G., D.S.O., and his staff for their unremitting efforts during the whole period to make our advance, as it was, rapid and decisive. To them are mainly due the excellent organisation and dispositions which ensured success without delay, and, above all, the perfection of arrangements for maintaining the troops in a waterless district far ahead of the railway, without which the dash and endurance of our troops would have been of no avail. The foresight, rapid decision and excellent arrangements of General Sir P. Chetwode and the staff of the Desert Column, the skilful leadership of General Chauvel, the cheerful endurance by the troops concerned of the fatigue and hardships entailed by the Magdhaba operations, and their gallantry and dash at Magruntein, are also worthy of the highest praise. During the actions the work of the Royal Flying Corps in co-operation with the mounted troops was admirable. Not only were the enemy harassed with bombs and machine-gun fire

throughout, but the aircraft reconnaissance was as reliable as it was untiring. General Chauvel and General Chetwode were kept constantly and accurately informed both of the enemy's movements and of the progress of their own widely dispersed troops, and the co-operation of the aircraft with the artillery was excellent. During the engagement at Magruntein the Royal Flying Corps, besides attacking the entrenched enemy and his relieving column, made a very successful raid on Beersheba.

11. As a result of the action near Rafa the enemy immediately began to concentrate his forces near Shellal, west of which place he began rapidly to prepare a strong defensive position near Weli Sheikh Nuran, with the object of covering his lines of communication and supply along the railway running into Beersheba from the north, and along the Jerusalem—Hebron—Beersheba road. The preparation of this position has continued up to the present date. During the earlier portion of January considerable activity was shown by the enemy's aircraft, both in reconnaissance and small bombing raids. On the other hand, the effect of our recent success on his moral was proved by the very marked increase in the number of deserters who came into our lines.

In the meantime arrangements had been progressing with a view to the concentration of additional troops towards El Arish, advantage being taken of the altered military situation in the south to reduce the number of troops allotted to the direct defences of the Suez Canal. During the first week in January the 53rd Division was concentrated complete at Romani. By the 13th January the 54th Division had been withdrawn altogether from the Southern Canal Section, and was concentrated at Moascar, ready to move north as soon as might be required. In order to relieve the Desert Column as far as possible from pre-occupation rearward, the eastern boundary of the Northern Canal Section was successively moved forward to the neighbourhood of Mazar on 3rd January, and to just west of Ujret el Zol on 24th January.

In the Southern Canal Section the only operation to record was the emptying and blocking of all except one of the rock cisterns in the Wadi um Muksheib, which had filled with water owing to recent rains. These measures were taken to ensure that lack of water should prevent an enemy force of any size from moving against the Canal by one of the southern routes.

Towards the end of January, in accordance with your Lordship's instructions, I made arrangements to concentrate the 42nd Division with a view to its despatch overseas. At the end of the month, accordingly, this division started from El Arish for Moascar, while the 53rd Division moved forward to El Arish in its place, and the 54th Division started from Moascar for Mazar. In general, the period following the action at Magruntein was, on my eastern front, devoted to preparations for a further advance. During the latter half of January a large supply depôt had been formed at El Arish with a view to building up at that place an advanced base of sufficient size to support the operations of three divisions and a mounted division of five or six brigades. After the railway reached El Arish a very large amount of work was found to be necessary in connection with the construction of a station of sufficient size. For a considerable time, therefore,—while this work was still incomplete—it was impossible to run supplies into El Arish itself by rail. Stores and supplies had to be detrained at Masaid and carried forward on camels, which necessarily increased the difficulties and delays. Invaluable work was done during this period, however, by the Royal Navy, in transporting and landing supplies from the sea at El Arish whenever the weather made this possible. The coast is exceptionally unfavourable for operations of this kind, owing to strong currents, a shelving and shifting beach, and heavy surf. Nevertheless, owing to the whole-hearted co-operation of Vice-Admiral Sir R. E. Wemyss, K.C.B., C.M.G., M.V.O., and those under him, a large amount of stores and supplies was landed; and, in the earlier portion of the period, during which our difficulties were at their greatest, the total reserve of supplies at El Arish almost exactly corresponded with the amount which had been landed from the sea. Before the end of the month the railway station at El Arish was completed, and sea transport of stores and supplies, being no longer necessary, was eventually discontinued. By the 31st January the forward construction of the railway had been resumed, and the track had been laid to a point 1,000 yards east of El Arish station.

12. During the month of February, on the eastern front, the railway, in spite of many difficulties owing to the heavy sand, was gradually pushed out along the coast from El Arish, till by the end of the month it was just short of Sheikh Zowaid. The period generally was devoted to the perfection of the El Arish position, and to energetic training of the troops. Our cavalry patrols kept the country up to and beyond Rafa continuously under observation, and steps were taken to bring in the local Bedouins who were becoming troublesome.

On 23rd February, deserters having given information that Khan Yunus had been evacuated, a reconnaissance was carried out against that place by the New Zealand Mounted Rifles Brigade. The column, arriving at dawn, found the position strongly held, and, after manœuvring the enemy out of his front line of defence and capturing prisoners, withdrew without difficulty. Continuous pressure maintained by our troops in this neighbourhood, however, induced the enemy to withdraw the garrison of Khan Yunus, which was entered by our cavalry without opposition on 28th February.

On 20th February, General Dobell transferred his headquarters to El Arish.

During the month also a successful minor operation was carried out in the interior of the Sinai Peninsula. Information having been received that the enemy had re-established small posts at Hassana and Nekhl, with the object of regaining his prestige in the eyes of the Bedouins, I ordered a combined operation against those two places to be undertaken by three mobile columns of cavalry and camelry, one column starting from El Arish against Hassana, and two starting from Serapeum and Suez respectively against Nekhl. The advance was so timed that all the columns should arrive at their destinations at dawn on 18th February. The column from El Arish, which reached Lahfan on the 16th, surrounded Hassana by daybreak on the 18th. The garrison of three officers and 19 other ranks at once surrendered without resistance. The town was searched, and a few camels, 21 rifles, and 2,400 rounds of small arms ammunition were found.

The northernmost of the Nekhl columns, leaving its point of concentration, some 25 miles east of the

THIRD DESPATCH

Great Bitter Lake, on the 14th, marched through the W. el Baha Pass to Bir el Themada, 25 miles north-west of Nekhl, where it arrived on the 16th. On the following day a patrol sent forward towards the Nekhl—Hassana road was fired on from the hills, and in the afternoon it was further reported that the road was clear and that men could be seen leaving Nekhl in an easterly direction. The advanced patrol captured four of the enemy and ten camels, but was prevented from crossing the plain east of Nekhl by rifle fire from about 50 of the enemy who had temporarily halted in the foothills on the Nekhl—Akaba (see Map 2) road. Nekhl was entered that evening by a squadron of the 11th Australian Light Horse Regiment, who captured two Bedouins and one Turk, the town being otherwise empty. Further pursuit of the enemy was impossible owing to darkness, and the remnants of the garrison were able to make good their escape eastwards along the waterless road towards Akaba. The main body entered Nekhl at dawn on the 18th, and the Southern Column from Suez reached the town at 9 a.m. The latter column, which included detachments of Indian infantry, had marched from Bir Abu Tif (20 miles south-east of Suez) through the difficult W. Abu Garawid pass to Ain Sudr and thence to Nekhl. The total captures at Nekhl were 11 prisoners, one field gun, a number of rifles, 16,000 rounds of small arms ammunition, 250 rounds of gun ammunition, and a quantity of stores and explosives. These well-executed and carefully-organised operations gave one more proof to the enemy of the mobility of our mounted troops, and of their power to strike over considerable stretches of waterless desert. The excellent arrangements for the Nekhl operation reflect great credit on

Brigadier-General P. C. Palin, C.B., General Officer Commanding, Southern Canal Section, and his staff.

13. During most of the period under review the western front had been quiet. My advance to the Baharia and Dakhla oases was accomplished without opposition, and the subsequent task on that front was that of policing its large area and guarding against the possibility of further raids on the part of the Senoussi with the minimum number of troops, so that as many as possible might be set free for operations on the eastern front.

On 4th October Major-General W. A. Watson, C.B., C.I.E., took over the command of the Western Force. By this date a column had already been concentrated at Shusha, three miles west of Samalut, for the purpose of conducting operations in the Baharia oasis. A few days later, however, reliable intelligence was received to the effect that Sayed Ahmed, who had already left the Dakhla oasis for Baharia, had left Baharia for Siwa on 9th October, the majority of his force preceding him, the rearguard following on the next day. It is probable that the news of my impending advance and the sickness and lack of food in the oasis, which impaired the moral of his troops, were deciding factors in determining his retreat. An immediate endeavour to intercept the enemy's rearguard was made by concentrating all available light armed cars west of Baharia, but the distance to be covered and the sandy nature of the country prevented the success of the attempt. Small mobile columns were at once pushed into the oases of Baharia (110 miles west of Samalut) and Dakhla (75 miles west of Kharga), and all the enemy who had not accompanied the retreat, some 300 in number, were captured with little resistance. The Harra wells, on the edge of the Baharia oasis, were captured by a detachment of the Imperial Camel Corps on the 17th, and on the 19th a detachment of the same corps entered the oasis and took possession of the villages of Harra, Mendisha, Bawitti, and Kasr. By the 21st, this oasis was completely in our possession, and the Baharia railway, which reached its terminus on the same date, commenced receiving traffic on the 23rd. A light car patrol and a detachment of Imperial Camel Corps, starting from Kharga on the 15th October, covered 70 miles of desert, and occupied Tenida in the Dakhla oasis by the 17th. The light cars pushed on to Budkhulu, capturing a tabur of 45 men and 10 camels, and on the 19th the Camel Corps detachment reached Bir Sheikh Mohammed, five miles west of Kasr Dakhla, and captured 40 more prisoners. From the 20th to the 22nd, a thorough "drive" was made of the oasis, with a systematic search of the villages, which resulted in the capture of 50 more of the enemy, besides many political prisoners. By the end of the month the oasis was entirely clear of the enemy.

During the following month permanent garrisons were established in these two oases. The Baharia garrison marched out on 6th November and encamped on the escarpment at Legalit Gate, where a very healthy site has been found. The inhabitants, who were undoubtedly glad to be rid of the Senoussi, all turned out to welcome the troops, and so far throughout the oasis the latter have always been well received. General Watson himself visited the oasis on 16th November, and held a durbar on the 17th at Bawitti, which was attended by the omdas, sheikhs and principal inhabitants. The Union Jack was hoisted in the presence of a guard of honour. On 15th November a patrol left

Legalit to reconnoitre the Farafra oasis. The town of Farafra was entered on the 19th. All Senoussi followers were separated from the inhabitants, and a search made for arms, with the result that 18 Senoussi prisoners and 12 rifles were taken. The patrol left Farafra on the 20th.

The successful operation of these two oases enabled me to commence reducing the Western Force to the limits necessary for maintaining security along the front, the chief units to be transferred to the eastern front being one brigade of dismounted, and two brigades of mounted, yeomanry, with two batteries of horse artillery. During December, General Watson visited Dakhla and held a durbar on the 19th. The task of reinstituting civil administration in both the Baharia and Dakhla oases has now been taken over by the civil authorities to the gratification of the inhabitants, and trade is being encouraged as much as possible. British troops have now been entirely withdrawn from Dakhla, while the Baharia oasis is held by a small mobile force of Camel Corps and motor patrols.

In the other sections of the western front the work done by the light and armoured cars, owing to the dash and enterprise of their officers, has been uniformly excellent. They are the terror of all the ill-disposed in the Western Desert, and to them, as much as to any, is due the satisfactory state of things which exists throughout from the coast down to the Fayum. The geographical information obtained by these patrols is also invaluable.

14. During October, under the direction of the Italian authorities, a combined British and Italian naval reconnaissance was carried out at El Ageila, 32 miles west of Mersa Tebruk, where a large camp of fol-

lowers of Idris and Nuri, with guns and a quantity of ammunition, was reported. The camp was shelled, serious casualties being inflicted. On 27th October a light armoured car patrol, accompanied by Lieut. Tescione, of the Italian Army, reconnoitred an enemy camp at Zowia Jansur, the Muhafzia holding the camp being driven off into the sand dunes by machine-gun fire. During November and December much valuable information of the desert routes in the Coastal Section was obtained by patrols. In the Moghara Section several attempts were made by the light car patrols to find a practicable route to the El Qara oasis, but the boggy ground and high sand dunes on each occasion defeated the attempt. Towards the end of November an interesting and useful reconnaissance was made from Assuan through the Kurkur oasis to Beris on the southernmost end of the Kharga oasis. The total distance covered was 336 miles.

15. During the month of January, I received intelligence that Sayed Ahmed, the Grand Senoussi, with his Commander-in-Chief, Mohammed Saleh, whose force amounted to some 1,200 men, were making preparations to depart from the Siwa oasis and to retire to Jaghbub. With the intention of capturing Sayed Ahmed, if possible, and of inflicting as much loss as possible on his followers, I gave orders on the 21st January that operations were to be undertaken against the Siwa and Girba oases (see map) at the earliest possible moment by a mixed force to consist of Imperial Camel Companies and armoured cars. Preparations for the march of such a force, however, over the 200 miles of waterless desert, between Mersa Matruh and Siwa, would have taken at least one month, and the expenditure of so much time was put out of the question by a

reliable report received towards the end of the month that Sayed Ahmed and his followers were on the point of leaving Siwa. I therefore ordered an immediate reconnaissance of the Siwa and Girba oases to be undertaken by a column consisting entirely of armoured motor-cars, and supplied by motor transport based on Mersa Matruh, with the object of verifying the above report and of inflicting as much loss as possible on such part of the enemy forces as might be met with. Command of this column was entrusted to Brigadier-General H. W. Hodgson, C.V.O., C.B., whose plan was to attack the enemy camp at Girba with his main body, and to detach two armoured motor batteries to block the pass at Garet el Munasib—the only pass between Siwa and Jaghbub practicable for camels—so that should Sayed Ahmed, as was probable, take to flight, casualties might be inflicted on his retreating column by the detached batteries, and his march be deflected into the waterless sand dunes.

16. The fighting force of three light armoured batteries and three light car patrols, each patrol of six Ford cars, was concentrated at Mersa Matruh by the evening of the 29th January. Owing, however, to a severe sandstorm, some of the heavy lorries of the heavy supply column did not arrive there from Dhabba till the 31st. The light supply column of 40 Ford vans moved out from Mersa Matruh on the same day, and the fighting force moved out early the following morning. The column, having halted for the night on the road, moved on the morning of the 2nd February to the point of concentration half-way between Gebel Lamlaz and Neqb el Shegga pass, 185 miles from Matruh. This long march over the desert track was carried out in good time, and all units reached the point

MAP of SIWA OASIS

THIRD DESPATCH

of concentration by 12 o'clock. After a reconnaissance towards the Siwa oasis, orders were given for an advance on Girba—at the western end of the Siwa oasis—on the following day, and for the move of the detachment allotted to block the Munasib pass.

By 9 a.m. on 3rd February all units had successfully descended the pass north-east of Girba and moved off to the attack, the advanced guard being divided into three parties of two armoured cars each, one of which was to attack each of the three enemy camps already located. The enemy was located in rough ground close under the rocky escarpment; he was completely surprised by the arrival of the armoured cars, and thrown into considerable confusion. Brisk fire was opened on the enemy, who at once took to the cliffs and rocks beyond the camps and returned our fire. The advanced guard was now reinforced, but, owing to the very rough nature of the country, it was impossible for the cars to approach nearer than a distance of 800 yards from the enemy without serious risk of getting stuck. As the action progressed, it became evident that the enemy, who was engaging the armoured cars with two guns and two machine guns, was in considerable force and did not intend to retire without a fight. Information obtained from deserters showed that the strength of the enemy at Girba was 850, while Sayed Ahmed, Mohammed Saleh and some 400 or 500 men were at Siwa. As afterwards appeared, Mohammed Saleh left to take command at Girba at the beginning of the engagement, while Sayed Ahmed and his force made off to the westward. General Hodgson, who made skilful arrangements for extricating his force, in case of a threat directed by the Siwa party on his left flank and rear, continued the action all day. The light armoured cars, though unable to get closer than 400 yards from the enemy's position, kept the enemy under an accurate fire, inflicting some casualties. Towards evening, the enemy's fire died down, though occasional bursts were fired from his machine guns during the night.

At 5 a.m. on the 4th February, the enemy fired four final rounds from his guns and several bursts of machine-gun fire. Fires were seen beyond his camp, movements of men and animals could be distinguished, and the sound of small-arms ammunition being burnt was heard. By dawn he had completely evacuated his position. The rest of the day was spent in destroying the enemy's camp, reconnoitring towards Siwa and resting the troops, and on the following morning, 5th February, the column entered Siwa without opposition. A parade, at which the local sheikhs were assembled, was held before the court-house, and a salute of nine guns fired with a Krupp gun that had been brought from Matruh in a motor lorry. Arrangements were then made for the collection of all rifles and for the repair of the passes leading down to the escarpment. The reception given to our troops by the inhabitants of the oasis was friendly, and reports from them confirmed the fact that the enemy had incurred considerable casualties. The column left the town on the same afternoon, and reached the point of concentration on the following day.

Meanwhile, the Munasib detachment, consisting of three armoured cars and a light car patrol, had reached its position on the evening of the 3rd February. It was found impossible to get the armoured cars down the steep escarpment, and they were forced to remain at a point 18 miles north of Munasib during the operations.

THIRD DESPATCH

The light car patrol and one Ford car managed to get down the escarpment and take up a position at Munasib. On the 4th this detachment captured a small convoy of mail-bags proceeding east to Siwa, and on the 5th it was able to intercept and cut up the leading parties of the enemy retreating from Girba. Subsequently, the enemy established a post out of reach of the cars, and warned all subsequent parties of the enemy to turn into the sand dunes before reaching the pass. The detachment was therefore ordered to return to the point of concentration, as there was no chance of further successful action. The whole column returned to Matruh on the 8th February, having sustained no casualties to personnel beyond three officers slightly wounded, or to material besides the loss of one tender with broken springs. The enemy's losses were 40 killed, including two Senoussi officers, and 200 wounded, including five Turkish officers; 70 rifles were brought in and 150 destroyed; 3,000 rounds of small-arms ammunition were brought in and 2,000 destroyed, besides what was burnt by the enemy; 40 of the enemy's camels were killed, and a large number of shelters and tents were burnt.

17. Though the capture of Sayed Ahmed and Mohammed Saleh was wanting to the complete success of the operations, the fighting troops—supported most admirably by the supply column working under extremely arduous conditions—accomplished all that was possible under the circumstances, and great credit is due to General Hodgson and his staff. The expedition, which, at my request, was accompanied by Captain Caccia, the Italian Military Attaché, dealt a rude blow to the moral of the Senoussi, left the Grand Senoussi himself painfully making his way to Jaghbub through

the rugged and waterless dunes, and freed my western front from the menace of his forces.

On 14th February, No. 2 Light Armoured Car Battery left Sollum to reconnoitre the road to Melfa. During this reconnaissance two enemy caravans were met and destroyed.

Preparations are now being made to maintain a small force in a fortified camp a few miles north of the Siwa oasis, in order to protect the inhabitants, and deal with any raiding parties of the enemy that may appear. At the same time, as a result of the above operations, I have been able to make a considerable further reduction in the fighting troops on the western front for the benefit of the eastern theatre.

18. The outstanding features of the period covered by this despatch have been, on the eastern front the rapid progress of the railways, and on the western front the work of the armoured cars. For the speed at which the railway has been pushed out along the desert to El Arish and beyond, the greatest credit is due to Colonel Sir G. Macauley, K.C.M.G., C.B., Director of Railways, the officers of his staff, and the officers and men of the railway companies. In spite of endless difficulties owing to heavy sand and lack of water, they maintained, by their strenuous efforts, a rate of advance which was not far behind that of the fighting troops, and were largely instrumental in enabling the latter to keep the enemy under a continual pressure.

I have already referred to the excellent work of the armoured cars and light car patrols on the western front. Their mobility, and the skill and energy with which they are handled, have made them an ideal arm for the Western Desert, where the sand is not so heavy as on the east. It is not too much to say that the successful clearance of the western oases, and the satisfactory state of affairs which now exists on the western front, is due more to the dash and enterprise of the armoured car batteries and the light car patrols than to any other cause, and the enemy has found many times to his cost that their range of action is far beyond that of any troops mounted on horses or camels.

The work of the Imperial Camel Corps has been excellent throughout. Three battalions of this corps have now been organised into a brigade, to which the Hong Kong and Singapore Mountain Battery has been attached. This brigade has formed a most valuable unit for operations on the eastern front. The Imperial Camel Corps includes Australian, New Zealand and Imperial units, and the efficiency of the camel companies is largely due to the efforts of the instructional staff at the headquarters of the corps at Abbassia, which has been continuously engaged in their training.

A great deal of the work of supplying the troops on both fronts has been done by the Camel Transport Corps, a unit which has been raised in this country since the commencement of operations, and which has invariably carried out its duties with the utmost efficiency.

The execution of the enormous amount of work necessitated by our advance on the eastern front would have been quite impossible had it not been for the Egyptian Labour Corps, which began to be recruited in this country early in 1916, and has now been increased to nearly 50,000 men, with recruiting depôts, rest camps, and administrative centres of its own. The officers of this corps have been largely found among gentlemen who are resident in this country, and were familiar with the language and customs of the population. The work of the Egyptian Labour Corps has not only been invaluable in this country, but detachments of it, sent to other theatres of war, have already won the highest appreciation.

My relations with the High Commissioner-General, Sir F. R. Wingate, G.C.B., G.C.V.O., K.C.M.G., D.S.O., have always been most cordial, and I should like to convey my gratitude for his ready assistance and valuable advice, which have always been at my disposal.

Now that the service of King's Messengers from England to Egypt has been discontinued, I wish to express my grateful appreciation of the services of all the officers employed in this responsible work. The risks involved were not small, as is proved by the fact that one officer was drowned, and another, when his ship was torpedoed, was forced to sink his despatches; nevertheless, this duty has always been faithfully and efficiently performed.

I have, in a former despatch, referred to the admirable work of the Red Cross and Order of St. John in this country, under the direction of Sir Courtauld Thomson, C.B. I desire now to express my obligation to those ladies and gentlemen who have given voluntary aid in connection with these institutions, and who have worked with a devotion deserving of the highest praise, in the interests of the sick and wounded. Not only have they earned the gratitude of the individuals they looked after, but also they deserve the thanks of their country, as they have materially contributed towards the rapid convalescence and, therefore, to the maintenance of the fighting efficiency of the Forces under my command.

THIRD DESPATCH

The operations which I have had the honour to describe in this despatch, and which have resulted in the freeing of Egyptian territory of all formed bodies of the enemy, could not have been successfully carried out by the Forces in the field, but for the devotion, energy and skill of the Headquarters Staff and Heads of the Administrative Services.

I have on previous occasions expressed my appreciation of the able manner in which Major-General A. L. Lynden-Bell, C.B., C.M.G., Chief of the General Staff, has discharged his duties. I wish again to bring this officer prominently to notice for his admirable work during the period under review.

The abolition of the Inspector-Generalship, Lines of Communication, has thrown upon my Deputy Quartermaster-General, Major-General W. Campbell, C.B., D.S.O., and my Deputy Adjutant-General, Major-General J. Adye, C.B., the whole of the work previously performed by the Inspector-General of Communications, and these duties they have had to discharge in addition to the normal work in connection with an army in the field. Moreover, my chief base at Alexandria is not only the base for the supply of the forces under my command, but is practically a clearing-house for stores for all campaigns in the East. The eastward advance has also now lengthened the lines of communication to something like 200 miles. I wish, therefore, specially to acknowledge the excellent work done by these two officers, and I shall have the pleasure of bringing before you the names of a number of officers of the Administrative Services in this connection.

I wish to bring to your notice the excellent manner in which my Assistant Military Secretary, Lieut.-

Colonel S. H. Pollen, C.M.G., has performed the exceptionally heavy work of his department.

A list of those officers, non-commissioned officers and men whom I desire to bring to your special notice in connection with these operations will be forwarded at an early date.

>I have the honour to be
>>Your Lordship's most obedient Servant,
>>>(Signed) A. J. MURRAY, General,
>>>>Commander-in-Chief,
>>>>>Egyptian Expeditionary Force.

FOURTH DESPATCH

28th June, 1917

LIEUTENANT-GENERAL SIR P. W. CHETWODE, BART., K.C.M.G., C.B., D.S.O.

FOURTH DESPATCH

From—
    The General Officer Commanding-in-Chief,
        Egyptian Expeditionary Force.

To—
    The Secretary of State for War,
        War Office, London, S.W.

                General Headquarters,
                      Egyptian Expeditionary Force,
                            28th June, 1917.

My Lord,

    I have the honour to submit a report on the operations of the Force under my command from 1st March to 28th June, 1917.

    1. Before entering into a detailed account of the operations during this period, the main events of which were the enemy's voluntary retirement from his position at Weli Sheikh Nuran and the two battles in front of Gaza, I think it necessary to point out that the policy of the War Cabinet, as communicated to me in instructions from the War Office, underwent several changes between the end of 1916 and April, 1917. In October, 1916,[1] I was informed that the policy in Egypt was to be mainly defensive, though it was hoped that all preparations were being made for an advance on El Arish. With this policy, including the plan of occupying, if possible, El Arish, I agreed,[2] though I stated at the

[1] W.O. letter 01/45/151, 4.10.16.
[2] My letter, No. G.S.Z./33/1, 21.10.16.

same time that my previous estimate of the number of troops necessary for holding and operating from El Arish—namely, five divisions and at least four mounted brigades—still held good, but that with the four divisions then at my disposal, the 42nd, 52nd, 53rd and 54th, I was prepared to defend Egypt and undertake the advance on El Arish. This advance, as I reported in my despatch of 1st March, 1917, was successfully accomplished by the end of December.

Meanwhile, early in the month of December, I was asked by telegram[1] to send my proposals for action beyond El Arish, and to state the additional troops which I should require to carry them out; and it was pointed out to me that the gaining of a military success in this theatre was very desirable. In my reply[2] I asked that two divisions might be sent to me, and, if possible, some more mounted troops. A further telegram[3] was sent to me on 12th December, instructing me to make the maximum effort possible during the winter, and inquiring when the two divisions for which I had asked would be required. I replied[4] that, while I was prepared to attempt the advance to Rafa with only four divisions, I considered that one additional division was now necessary to ensure security and to hold, and operate from, El Arish—thus once more repeating my original estimate that five divisions would be required for this purpose—and that another division would be needed, not before 15th February, for a further advance from Rafa towards Palestine. At the same time I forwarded[5] in detail the plan on which I have since worked for my

---

[1] W.O. telegram, No. 26174, cipher, 9.12.16.
[2] My telegram, No. A.M. 1380, 10.12.16.
[3] W.O. telegram, No. 26289, cipher, 12.12.16.
[4] My telegram, No. A.M. 1389, 13.12.16.
[5] My letter, G.S.Z./33/1, 13.12.16.

further advance along the sea coast into Palestine. The next communication[1] which I received (dated 15th December) indicated that the War Cabinet were not prepared to give me the troops asked for. I was informed that, notwithstanding recent instructions to make the maximum effort possible during the winter, my primary mission was the defence of Egypt, and that I should be notified if and when the War Cabinet changed this policy. I was further informed that no more mounted troops could be sent, and that the possibility of my getting two more divisions depended on whether they could be released from another theatre of war. No further indications of policy were given me till after the occupation of El Arish, but early in January it appeared that the War Cabinet had decided to make everything subsidiary to the concentration of strong forces in France. A telegram[2] of 11th January informed me that the War Cabinet had decided that, as the general situation would not permit of sending out the reinforcements for which I had asked, the undertaking of any operations in Palestine on a large scale should be postponed until the autumn, and that, while preparing for this campaign during the summer, I was to be ready to release one or two divisions for France. A few days later, definite instructions arrived[3] to send a division to France, acting on which I withdrew the 42nd Division —then the best in my force—forthwith, and it sailed early in March. This indication of a changed policy was confirmed by a letter[4] of 11th January, in which I was informed of the acceptance by the War Cabinet in principle of an autumn campaign in Palestine, and

[1] W.O. telegram, No. 26624, cipher, 15.12.16.
[2] W.O. telegram, No. 27761, cipher, 11.1.17.
[3] W.O. telegram, No. 28297, cipher, 22.1.17.
[4] W.O. letter 01/45/151, 11.1.17.

instructed that my primary mission, after the occupation of Rafa, was the defence of Egypt during the summer months and the preparation of an offensive campaign in the autumn. In reply[1] to this, I again stated that I adhered to my estimate of the need of five divisions to safeguard Egypt, hold El Arish, and protect the Suez Canal.

Between the end of January and the end of March, though I was now reduced to three infantry divisions, I made every effort as far as possible to keep up the offensive. Owing to the satisfactory state of affairs in the Canal defences and in the west, I was now able to employ all three of my divisions on the eastern front, to concentrate all my mounted troops in two mounted divisions, and to commence the formation of the 74th Division from the dismounted yeomanry brigades in the force. Several months, however, were bound to elapse before this division could be completely equipped, efficiently trained and supplied with its full complement of divisional troops. Early in March, to my disappointment, the enemy, whom I had every hope of successfully attacking in his position at Weli Sheikh Nuran, evacuated this position before our troops were within reach of him. It was to prevent a repetition of these tactics and to bring the Turks to fight that I determined to attack the Gaza position as soon as possible, considering that the advantage of thus exerting pressure on the enemy, and possibly taking Gaza by a *coup de main*, would outweigh the risk of making the attack in a waterless country considerably in advance of rail-head.

Though the *coup de main* just failed, the military results of the first battle of Gaza, in my opinion, justified my anticipations. The enemy was brought to fight,

[1] My letter G.S.Z./33/1, 30.1.17.

FOURTH DESPATCH

losing heavily in killed and wounded, and the advance of the railway to Wadi Ghuzze was assured. It was at this time, the end of March, when the hitherto adverse situation in Mesopotamia was rapidly changing in our favour, that the War Cabinet again changed the policy in this theatre. In a telegraphic communication[1] dated 30th March, I was instructed, in view of the altered situation, to make my object the defeat of the Turks south of Jerusalem and the occupation of Jerusalem. I replied,[2] drawing attention once more to my never-varying estimate of the troops required, that a rapid advance could not be expected unless I were fortunate enough to inflict a severe blow on the enemy, and that heavy fighting with considerable losses would have to be expected if the Turks held, as I anticipated, a series of strong positions between the Gaza—Beersheba and the Jerusalem—Jaffa lines. After consideration of this reply by the War Cabinet, I was informed[3] that the War Cabinet relied on me to pursue the enemy with all the rapidity compatible with the necessary progress of my communications, and was anxious that I should push my operations with all energy, though at the same time no additional troops were to be sent to me, since it was considered that, in view of the military situation of the enemy, my present force would suffice. At that time, as always, I had fully appreciated the importance of offensive operations in this theatre, and, having failed to take Gaza by a *coup de main*, I was anxious to take it, if possible, by more deliberate operations before the enemy was further reinforced, chiefly on account of its water-supply. I was therefore ready, as I stated at the time, to attack Gaza with my present

[1] W.O. telegram, No. 31854, cipher, 30.3.17.
[2] My telegram, No. A.M. 1749, 31.3.17.
[3] W.O. telegram, No. 31955, cipher, 1.4.17, No. 32017, cipher, 2.4.17.

force before the end of April, and had good hopes, provided the enemy was not heavily reinforced, of capturing that town.

The second battle of Gaza took place between the 17th and 20th April. I succeeded in pushing on to within a mile or two of the town, but was unable to take the key of the position, Ali el Muntar. The enemy force in front of me was then five divisions, with considerably increased numbers of Austrian and German gunners and machine-gunners, and it was abundantly clear that, owing to the relaxation of pressure further east, the Turks had been able to reinforce their units heavily from depôts in the north of Palestine.

When, therefore, after the second battle of Gaza, I was asked[1] to state my requirements for a continuation of the offensive, I replied[2] that my estimate of five fully-equipped and complete divisions still held good, whereas, at present, I had only three considerably depleted by recent fighting, one just formed and incompletely trained, and six battalions—the majority far from fit—towards the formation of a fifth division. My requirements, therefore, were two complete divisions and enough field artillery to complete all divisions to a normal scale. With the troops which I had at the time I could hope for no more than a local success. In view of this position and the inability of the Russian Army in the Caucasus to relieve the pressure, the War Cabinet decided to change the policy, and at the end of April I was informed[3] that Jerusalem was no longer my objective, but that my mission for the present was to take favourable opportunity of defeating the Turkish forces opposed to me and to follow up any success

---

[1] W.O. telegram, No. 33191, cipher, 21.4.17.
[2] My telegram, No. O. 328, 22.4.17.
[3] W.O. telegram, No. 33394, cipher, 25.4.17.

gained with all the means at my disposal. To this task I devoted my energies throughout the month of May, during which time I was engaged in broadening my front by laying down branch railway and pipe-lines from Rafa eastwards and south-eastwards to the Wadi Ghuzze, so that I might eventually effectually threaten Beersheba and the railway north of that place. Thanks to the unremitting labour of all concerned, in spite of immense difficulties, these preparations are now well advanced, and we are now in a position to take the offensive in any part of the line from Gaza to Beersheba, though the date of the offensive must depend upon when my deficit of 9,000 infantry can be made good by drafts, and when reinforcements can arrive from Salonica.

It would be of interest, as this is my last despatch, to review shortly here how the Egyptian Expeditionary Force has varied in strength between the beginning of 1916 and the present time.

At the end of January, 1916, besides a small portion of the 46th Division, there were in Egypt, either in the Egyptian Expeditionary Force or in the Force in Egypt, the Australian and New Zealand Mounted Division, three mounted yeomanry brigades, the Imperial Service Cavalry Brigade, and three double companies Bikanir Camel Corps, 11 infantry divisions (including the Australian and New Zealand troops), one Indian infantry division, three dismounted yeomanry brigades, two Territorial infantry brigades, two brigades of 60-pounders, and the equivalent of three brigades of siege artillery, besides garrison battalions and other minor units. The South African Infantry Brigade subsequently arrived in this country.

Between this time and the end of May, 1916, six

complete divisions at full strength, three infantry brigades, and nine batteries of heavy and siege artillery, besides certain signal, engineer and medical units, were embarked for service in other theatres. Meanwhile, the 4th and 5th Australian Divisions had been formed, the dismounted yeomanry organised in four brigades, six companies of the Imperial Camel Corps raised and trained, and the Camel Transport Corps raised to a strength of 18,000. So that in May, the Force in Egypt having now been amalgamated with the Egyptian Expeditionary Force, the following were the principal components of the Force :—One mounted division, three mounted yeomanry brigades, the Imperial Service Cavalry Brigade (less one regiment), six companies Imperial Camel Corps, six companies Bikanir Camel Corps, seven infantry divisions, four dismounted brigades, seven battalions of Indian infantry, three batteries of 60-pounders.

During June and July, 1916, the 4th and 5th Australian Divisions and the 11th Division embarked for France, thus bringing the total number of troops sent out of the country since January to 232,000, not including medical units. Between this time and the end of February, 1917, no material change took place in the composition of the Egyptian Expeditionary Force, save that three further companies, Bikanir Camel Corps, arrived, additional companies of the Camel Corps were raised (the total number of companies is now 18), the Camel Transport Corps was also considerably increased, and the Egyptian Labour Corps, the recruitment of which had begun early in 1916, had reached a total of nearly 50,000.

During the period covered by this report the 42nd Division has sailed for France, the 74th Division has been formed from three of the dismounted brigades (one having been previously disbanded), with the necessary divisional troops; the 75th Division has been formed from battalions that have arrived from India and elsewhere and Indian infantry battalions. The arrival of an additional mounted brigade from Salonica has enabled me to reorganise my mounted troops into three mounted divisions, each of three mounted brigades. One more mounted brigade and the 60th Division are in process of arrival from Salonica, and reinforcements of heavy artillery (some of which have already arrived) are *en route*. So that at the present the composition of the Egyptian Expeditionary Force, allowing for reorganisation now actually in progress, is :—Three mounted divisions (each of three brigades), four infantry divisions, one further infantry division in process of formation and one division *en route*, 18 companies Imperial Camel Corps, nine companies Bikanir Camel Corps, with a tenth now in process of formation; six batteries of 60-pounders, two siege batteries and a prospective total of $7\frac{1}{2}$ siege batteries of heavy howitzers. In other words, the present fighting units of the Egyptian Expeditionary Force, when all advised reinforcements have arrived, will form the equivalent of one cavalry corps and two infantry corps, with the necessary artillery.

Having thus summarised these main developments of policy and variations of strength, I now proceed to the more detailed narrative.

2. At the beginning of March the Eastern Force, under the command of Lieut.-General Sir Charles Dobell, K.C.B., C.M.G., D.S.O., was concentrated in the neighbourhood of El Arish. The headquarters of the Desert Column, under the command of Lieut.-

General Sir P. Chetwode, Bt., K.C.M.G., C.B., D.S.O., were at Sheikh Zowaid, in advance of which place the mounted troops of the column were covering the construction of the railway, which was being rapidly extended along the coast towards Rafa. Our mounted patrols, as I reported in my last despatch, had on 28th February entered the village of Khan Yunus, which had been evacuated by the enemy. Every preparation was being made for an attack in force on the strong position at Weli Sheikh Nuran, upon which the Turks had been working incessantly since the beginning of January. On 5th March, however, aeroplane reconnaissance established the fact that the enemy had decided not to face our attack and was evacuating this carefully prepared position. I at once instructed the General Officer Commanding, Eastern Force, to do all that was possible either to prevent this evacuation or to inflict loss on the enemy during its execution, and the Royal Flying Corps were ordered to carry out bomb attacks with the utmost energy against the enemy's communications. Accordingly, on 6th March and the following days vigorous attacks were made by our aircraft on the railway at Beersheba, Tel el Sharia and the junction station on the Jerusalem—Er Ramle line; but it was found impossible for our infantry or mounted troops to make any effective move against the enemy, owing to the distance between rail-head and Weli Sheikh Nuran. The enemy had retired while he was still out of reach, and his troops, which then consisted of about two divisions, were subsequently distributed between Gaza and Tel el Sharia, with a small garrison at Beersheba.

It thus became necessary to meet an altered situation, which was complicated by complete uncertainty

FOURTH DESPATCH

as to the line on which the enemy would ultimately elect to stand, and also to decide on the method and direction of my advance into Palestine. I decided that it would in any case be unwise to make an attempt on Beersheba, since by so doing I should be drawing my line of communications parallel to the enemy's front, and there was no technical advantage to be gained by linking up the military railway with the Central Palestine Railway, either at Beersheba or Tel el Sharia. The true line of advance was still along the coast, since the enemy was no less effectually threatened thereby, while my line of communications was more easily protected and railway construction was more rapid, owing to the absence of gradients. The coastal district, too, was better supplied with water. I decided therefore to continue for the present a methodical advance up the coast, moving troops forward as the railway could supply them, together with energetic preparation of the force for an attack in strength as soon as the state of its communications should make that possible. The most important thing was to increase the radius and mobility of the striking force. The Desert Column was therefore reconstituted to consist of the two cavalry divisions (each less one brigade) — the concentration of the Imperial Mounted Division, under Major-General H. W. Hodgson, C.V.O., C.B., being completed at Sheikh Zowaid by 16th March — and the 53rd Division, together with two light armoured motor batteries. Local arrangements were also made by which improvised trains, both of horses and camels, should be available for the three infantry and two cavalry divisions in the Eastern Force. At the same time, the Imperial Camel Corps Brigade was constituted as an independent unit of three battalions, Imperial Camel Corps, with a proportion of brigade troops, including the Hong Kong and Singapore Battery; and the three infantry brigades which had been formed out of the dismounted yeomanry regiments were combined into the 74th Division, under the command of Major-General E. S. B. Girdwood. This division, however, had no artillery or other divisional troops; its brigades had to be gradually collected from different parts of Egypt, and it needed a period of divisional training before it could take its place beside the three other infantry divisions in the force. Its headquarters arrived at El Arish on 6th March, and its first brigade at the same place on 8th March. I was enabled to form this division by the continued quietness of the western front, which made it possible to amalgamate the Delta District and Western Force into one command, which was entrusted to Brigadier-General H. G. Casson, C.M.G., and to garrison the posts on the western front entirely with garrison battalions, light armoured motor batteries and light car patrols, and the Bikanir Camel Corps.

3. By the middle of the month the railway had reached Rafa, and the work of making a large station there, with the requisite sidings, was being rapidly pushed on. The Desert Column was between Rafa and Sheikh Zowaid, the 52nd Division was at Sheikh Zowaid, and the 54th Division between that place and El Arish. There were distinct indications that the enemy intended to withdraw his troops without a fight from the Gaza—Tel el Sharia—Beersheba line, a move which it was highly important to prevent, while it was necessary to seize the line of the Wadi Ghuzze in order to protect the advance of the railway from Rafa towards Gaza. The chief difficulty lay in deciding, in view of these

considerations, the exact moment when it would be wise to abandon the methodical advance and to push out to its full radius of action a considerable force into a country bare of all supplies and almost devoid of water. I came to the conclusion that it would be necessary to push forward the Desert Column as soon as it could be supplied from Rafa Station, and the two other infantry divisions could be maintained in support of it between Rafa and the Wadi Ghuzze. It appeared that these conditions would be fulfilled shortly before the end of the month. I therefore instructed the General Officer Commanding, Eastern Force, to concentrate the Desert Column about Deir el Belah, a small village to the south-west of the Wadi Ghuzze, with one of the supporting divisions on the ridge to the east of Deir el Belah and the other in the neighbourhood of Khan Yunus, with the Imperial Camel Corps Brigade to cover the right flank of the force. When these dispositions were completed, the Desert Column, with the Imperial Camel Corps Brigade attached, was to march on Gaza, thus giving the enemy the alternative of standing his ground and fighting, or of submitting to the attacks of our cavalry on his flanks and rear, should he attempt to retire.

On the 20th March, General Dobell moved his headquarters to Rafa, whither, on the same day, Headquarters, Desert Column, moved from Sheikh Zowaid. The further preliminary moves, covered by the cavalry, who on the 23rd approached very near the outskirts of Gaza, were completed without any hitch by the 25th March. By the evening of that date the whole of the Desert Column were concentrated at Deir el Belah, the 54th Division was at In Seirat under the hills to the east of Deir el Belah, the 52nd Division at Khan

Yunus, and the Camel Corps Brigade and armoured batteries about Abasan el Kebir. All preliminary reconnaissances had been carried out, and the orders to the General Officer Commanding, Desert Column, were to advance on Gaza in the early hours of the following morning, the cavalry pushing out to the east and north of the town to block the enemy's lines of retreat, while the 53rd Division attacked Gaza in front. The 54th Division was to cross the Wadi Ghuzze in rear of the mounted troops of the Desert Column to a position of readiness in the neighbourhood of Sheikh Abbas, a commanding ridge five miles S.S.E. of Gaza, where a position was to be selected suitable for defence against an attack from east or south-east. One infantry brigade and one artillery brigade of this division were to assemble at a convenient point to the west of this position, where they would be held in readiness to reinforce the Desert Column at short notice. One brigade group of the 52nd Division was to be brought up to replace the 54th Division at In Seirat. The enemy's main body was in the Nejed — Huj area, south of the Wadi el Hesi, covered by detachments about Gaza, Sharia — Abu Hereira and Beersheba. His strength appeared to be between two and three divisions.

The object of this advance was three-fold: firstly, to seize the line of the Wadi Ghuzze to cover the advance of the railway; secondly, at all costs to prevent the enemy from retiring without a fight; thirdly, if possible, to capture Gaza by a *coup de main* and to cut off its garrison.

On 25th March I set up my Advanced General Headquarters at El Arish for the period of the operations, and on the following morning Battle Headquarters of Eastern Force were established just north of In Seirat.

4. Early in the morning of 26th March the preliminary movements were begun and successfully accomplished. The Australian and New Zealand Mounted Division left its bivouacs at 2.30 a.m. and crossed the Wadi Ghuzze, closely followed by the Imperial Mounted Division. The leading division headed for Beit Durdis, five miles east of Gaza, having completed its crossing of the Wadi by 6.15 a.m. The Imperial Mounted Division, after crossing the Wadi, headed due east for El Mendur, where it arrived at 9.30. The moves of the mounted divisions, as well as of the infantry, were considerably delayed by a very dense fog, which came on just before dawn and did not entirely clear till 8 a.m. This unavoidable delay had a serious effect upon the subsequent operations. The Imperial Camel Corps Brigade crossed the Wadi Ghuzze a little further south, and also proceeded to El Mendur, where its rôle was to assist the Imperial Mounted Division in observing the enemy in the direction of Huj and Hereira, and to withstand any attempts to relieve Gaza from those directions. At 9.30 a.m. the Australian and New Zealand Mounted Division reached Beit Durdis, and pushed out detachments to the west, north and east. In the course of these movements the 2nd Australian Light Horse Brigade closed the exit from Gaza and rested their right on the sea. A detachment of this brigade captured the Commander of the 53rd Turkish Division, with his staff, while he was driving into Gaza; also a convoy of 30 Turks. Later in the morning the same brigade destroyed the head of a Turkish column with machine-gun fire as it debouched from Gaza in a north-easterly

direction. The Imperial Mounted Division sent out patrols towards Hereira, Tel el Sharia and Huj, while two squadrons of the 5th Mounted Brigade were placed astride the Beersheba—Gaza road, about five miles south-east of Gaza, and one squadron was sent north to gain touch with the Australian and New Zealand Mounted Division. Later in the morning these squadrons found themselves engaged with enemy mounted troops, supported by bodies of infantry, and remained so throughout the day against continuously increasing numbers. They were also exposed to the fire of heavy guns at Hereira, and suffered some casualties in consequence.

Meanwhile, the 53rd Division, under the command of Major-General A. G. Dallas, C.B., C.M.G., having thrown forward strong bridge-heads before dawn, crossed the Wadi Ghuzze at a point some three miles from the sea-coast, with the 158th Brigade on the right directed on the Mansura ridge, and the 160th Brigade on the left directed on El Sheluf, some two miles south of Gaza on the ridge running south-west from that place. The 159th Brigade was held in reserve, and crossed in rear of 158th Brigade. The Gloucestershire Hussars, with a battalion and a section of 60-pounders, crossed the Wadi near the sea-coast, and for the remainder of the day successfully carried out their rôle of working up the sandhills to cover the left of the 53rd Division, and to keep the enemy employed between the village of Sheikh Ahmed and Gaza. At the same time the divisional squadron secured a good gun position and an excellent observation station for another section of 60-pounders on the far side of the Wadi Ghuzze, in the neighbourhood of the main road from Gaza to Khan Yunus. The 54th Division, under the command of Major-General S. W. Hare, C.B., began to cross the Wadi at 7 a.m., and the 162nd and 163rd Brigades proceeded to take up a defensive position on the Sheikh Abbas ridge, south-east of Gaza. These brigades remained in their positions throughout the day without coming into action. The 161st Brigade, with a brigade of field artillery, remained in the vicinity of the Wadi, so as to be at the disposal of the General Officer Commanding, 53rd Division, when required. During the morning this brigade was ordered to Mansura, to come under the orders of the General Officer Commanding, 53rd Division, and it finally assembled at that point about 3.30 in the afternoon. After the preliminary reconnaissances had been completed, the 53rd Division commenced to deploy from the line El Sheluf—Mansura, to attack the Ali Muntar position, with the following objectives :—The 160th Brigade astride the El Sheluf—Ali Muntar ridge on the enemy's south-western defences; the 158th Brigade moving north from Mansura on the prominent Ali Muntar ridge on the southern outskirts of the town; and the 159th Brigade, less one battalion in divisional reserve, pivoting on the right of the 158th Brigade on the hill 1,200 yards north-east of Ali Muntar, in co-operation with the attack of the 158th Brigade. The deployment of the 160th and 158th Brigades commenced at 11.50 a.m., and the 159th Brigade moved forward shortly afterwards to its assigned position. In cooperation with artillery fire and long-range machine-gun fire, the 160th Brigade pressed forward along the ridge, and the 158th and 159th Brigades over the flat, open ground, practically devoid of cover. The final advance, which began just after 1 p.m., was very steady, and all the troops behaved magnificently, though the enemy offered a very stout resistance, both with rifle and machine-gun fire, and our advancing troops, during the approach march, the deployment and attack, were subjected to a heavy shrapnel fire.

About 1 p.m., General Officer Commanding, Desert Column, decided to throw the whole of the Australian and New Zealand Mounted Division against the north and north-east of Gaza to assist the infantry. Both mounted divisions were placed under the orders of Major-General Sir H. G. Chauvel, K.C.M.G., C.B., General Officer Commanding, Australian and New Zealand Mounted Division, with instructions that he should bring the Imperial Mounted Division further north to continue observing the enemy, while the Imperial Camel Corps Brigade was ordered to conform to this movement and observe the country from the right of the Imperial Mounted Division. About the same time, considerable enemy activity was observed on the roads leading north and east of Tel el Sharia, and also about Hereira. By 3.30 p.m., General Chauvel had collected his division, with the exception of some detachments not yet relieved, and had commenced to move on Gaza, together with the 3rd Australian Light Horse Brigade from the Imperial Mounted Division. The attack was made with the 2nd Australian Light Horse Brigade on the right, with its right flank on the sea, the New Zealand Mounted Rifles Brigade in the centre directed on the continuation of the Ali Muntar ridge, and the 22nd Mounted Brigade, less one detachment, on the left, east of the town.

5. Meanwhile, the infantry attack was being pressed with great vigour, and by 4.30 p.m. considerable progress had been made. Portions of the enemy's positions were already in our hands, and shortly after-

wards the Ali Muntar hill, a strong work known as the Labyrinth, and the ground in the immediate neighbourhood, fell into our hands. The Australian and New Zealand Mounted Division was already exerting pressure on the enemy, and by 5 p.m. the enemy was holding out in the trenches, and on the hill south of the mosque only. The General Officer Commanding, 53rd Division, called on the 161st Brigade (Brigadier-General W. Marriott-Dodington), which had been placed at his disposal, to take this position. The brigade responded with the greatest gallantry in face of a heavy fire, and after some hard fighting, it pushed home its attack with complete success, so that, when darkness fell, the whole of the Ali Muntar position had been carried and a footing gained on the ridge to a point about 1,200 yards north-east of that position. Meanwhile, during the relief of the observing detachments of the Australian and New Zealand Mounted Division by the Imperial Mounted Division, the enemy, pressing his advance vigorously from the east, had succeeded in dislodging our troops from a prominent position on the east of Gaza. To restore the situation on this flank, General Chauvel sent back the 3rd Australian Light Horse Brigade. Thanks to the skilful leadership of Brigadier-General J. R. Royston, C.M.G., D.S.O., General Officer commanding this brigade, and his promptness in taking up his position, the mounted troops, supported by horse artillery and motor batteries, were able to prevent any further advance by the enemy from this direction. The attack of the Australian and New Zealand Mounted Division on the north of Gaza was pushed home with the greatest dash and gallantry, in conjunction with the infantry attack. The New Zealand Mounted Rifles Brigade were soon in possession of the redoubt of the ridge east of Gaza, while the 22nd Mounted Brigade on their left carried the knoll running west from that ridge. During these operations the Somerset Battery, Royal Horse Artillery, in support of the 2nd Australian Light Horse Brigade, silenced two enemy guns, and the New Zealand Mounted Rifles Brigade captured and retained, in spite of counter-attacks, two 77-mm. guns, which they used with skill on small bodies of the enemy which were still in the occupation of houses in the vicinity. As a result, 20 prisoners were taken, and eventually the guns were safely brought away. The whole division then established itself amongst the cactus hedges on the outskirts of the town, all brigades overcoming serious difficulties in fighting their way through the cactus hedges, in spite of the stubborn resistance of the enemy, the 2nd Australian Light Horse Brigade, under the command of Brigadier-General G. de L. Ryrie, C.M.G., particularly distinguishing itself in this phase of the operations.

6. When darkness fell, the situation was as follows: Gaza was enveloped, and the enemy, in addition to heavy losses in killed and wounded, had lost 700 prisoners. The 53rd Division was occupying the Ali Muntar position, which it had captured, but its right flank was very much in the air, only a thin line of cavalry holding off the relief columns of continually increasing strength which were approaching from north and east. In support of this division, the 54th Division, less one brigade, was holding Sheikh Abbas, with its left about $2\frac{1}{2}$ miles from the flank of the 53rd. The Australian and New Zealand Mounted Division was very much extended round Gaza, and was engaged in street fighting. The Imperial Mounted Division and the Imperial Camel Corps Brigade, on a very wide

front, were endeavouring to hold off enemy forces. The majority of the mounted troops had been unable to water their horses during the day, and it appeared that, unless Gaza was captured during the day, they would have to withdraw west of the Wadi Ghuzze in order to water their animals. Strong columns of the enemy, with guns, were moving to the relief of Gaza from the north, north-east and south-east. It was at this moment that the loss of two hours' daylight made itself particularly felt, since, had two more hours' daylight now been available, there is no doubt that the infantry would have been able to consolidate the positions they had won, and that arrangements could have been made by which the 54th Division could have effected junction with the 53rd. It is perhaps possible that, if General Dobell had, at this stage, pushed forward his reserve (the 52nd Division) to support the 53rd, the result would have been different, but the difficulty of supplying water for men and horses would have been immense, and impossible to realise by those who were not on the spot. As it was, after consultation with General Officer Commanding, Eastern Force, the General Officer Commanding, Desert Column, in order to prevent the envelopment of his mounted troops, decided to withdraw them during the night; he therefore directed General Chauvel to break off the engagement and retire his divisions west of the Wadi Ghuzze, using the Imperial Camel Corps Brigade to assist in his retirement. This movement made the maintenance by the 53rd Division of the very exposed position which it had captured no longer possible, and General Officer Commanding, Desert Column, reluctantly ordered General Officer Commanding, 53rd Division, to draw back his right and gain touch on that flank with the two remaining brigades of the 54th Division, which had already been ordered by General Officer Commanding, Eastern Force, to fall back westwards from Sheikh Abbas and take up a line on the El Burjaliya ridge, running south-westwards from Mansura, with their left in touch with the 161st Brigade, which was to fall back from its line south of Ali Muntar and establish an outpost line further back, with its right in touch with the remainder of the division. These movements were carried out during the night, the 53rd and 54th Divisions converging so that their inner (or northward) flanks rested one on the other, their lines running along the El Sire and El Burjaliya ridges respectively, the Imperial Camel Corps Brigade closing the gap between the right of the 54th Division and the Wadi Ghuzze. The retirement of the mounted troops was accomplished without difficulty, though, during the movement, the 3rd Australian Light Horse Brigade became engaged with the enemy advancing from the direction of Huj, but succeeded in driving them off with the assistance of No. 7 Light Car Patrol. At dawn on the 27th, the 11th and 12th Light Armoured Motor Batteries found themselves in the middle of a large body of the enemy, but brilliantly extricated themselves, causing considerable casualties to the enemy.

7. The withdrawal of the cavalry and the retirement of the 53rd Division on to the El Sire ridge, enabled the enemy to reinforce the garrison of Gaza with considerable bodies of troops. At daybreak, nevertheless, reconnoitring patrols from the 160th and 161st Brigades pushed forward and seized the positions up to and including the Ali Muntar hill, which had been captured on the day before. They encountered some resistance, but drove the enemy out and established

themselves on this line. At 8 a.m. the 53rd Division and the Imperial Camel Corps Brigade passed under the direct command of General Officer Commanding, Eastern Force. As soon as the advanced parties of infantry were established in the recaptured positions, preparations were made by the General Officer Commanding, 53rd Division, to reinforce them, but before the reinforcements could reach their objective, a strong counter-attack was made by fresh Turkish troops, which were pouring in from the north and north-east. This counter-attack drove our patrols out of the position on Ali Muntar Hill, though further advance from it on the part of the enemy was prevented by our artillery, and our infantry still held the rest of the positions. Since, however, the junction of the right of the 53rd Division and the left of the 54th made an acute salient exposed to attack on three sides, it was necessary to withdraw the line here, so as to eliminate the acute angle. In addition to the Turkish reinforcements coming from the east and north-east against Ali Muntar, another body appeared early in the morning on the Sheikh Abbas ridge, which they occupied. From this point they directed artillery fire on the rear of our positions on the Mansura ridge, doing a certain amount of damage among the transport animals, and making any movement of camel transport during the day impossible. Our positions were also exposed to heavy artillery fire from the north. Nevertheless, though tired and ill-supplied with water, the 53rd and 54th Divisions, now placed under the command of the General Officer Commanding, 53rd Division, remained throughout the day staunch and cheerful, and perfectly capable of repulsing, with heavy losses to the enemy, any Turkish counter-attacks. At no point was any enemy attack successful, and the Imperial Camel Corps, on the right of the 54th Division, in repulsing the attack by the 3rd Turkish Cavalry Division, practically annihilated the attackers. The position, however, was an impossible one to hold permanently. It was narrow and exposed to attack and artillery fire from three directions; also, it was devoid of water, and hostile artillery fire made the approach to it by day of slow-moving camel convoys with water and supplies impossible. If it had now been practicable for the General Officer Commanding, Eastern Force, to advance with his three infantry divisions and two cavalry divisions, I have no doubt that Gaza could have been taken, and the Turks forced to retire; but the reorganisation of the force for a deliberate attack would have taken a considerable time, the horses of the cavalry were very fatigued, and the distance of the rail-head from the front line put the immediate maintenance of such a force with supplies, water and ammunition entirely out of the question. The only alternative, therefore, was to retire the infantry, and this movement, after a strong counter-attack at 4 p.m. on the northern apex of our position had been shattered by our rifle, machine-gun and artillery fire, was carried out during the night at the order of General Officer Commanding, Eastern Force. By daylight the whole force had reached the western side of the Wadi Ghuzze and taken up a strong defensive position covering Deir el Belah. The enemy made no attempt to advance on the 28th, but contented himself with the occupation of the Gaza defences, our cavalry remaining in touch with him throughout the day. Arrangements were made on the 29th for the defensive line on the western side of the Wadi Ghuzze to be divided into sections, to be held by the 54th,

52nd and 53rd Divisions respectively, to cover the further progress of the railway, which was just reaching Khan Yunus.

8. The total of the first battle of Gaza, which gave us 950 Turkish and German prisoners and two Austrian field guns, caused the enemy losses which I estimate at 8,000, and cost us under 4,000 casualties, of which a large proportion were only slightly wounded, was that my primary and secondary objects were completely attained, but that the failure to attain the third object—the capture of Gaza—owing to the delay caused by fog on the 26th, and the waterless nature of the country round Gaza, prevented a most successful operation from being a complete disaster to the enemy. The troops engaged, both cavalry, camelry and infantry, especially the 53rd Division and the 161st Brigade of the 54th, which had not been seriously in action since the evacuation of Suvla Bay at the end of 1915, fought with the utmost gallantry and endurance, and showed to the full the splendid fighting qualities which they possess.

9. Preparations were immediately begun for a second attack in greater force on the Gaza positions as soon as possible, though I instructed the General Officer Commanding, Eastern Force, that upon no consideration was a premature attack to be made. At the same time, the utmost expedition was made necessary by the receipt of the instructions from the War Office to press on towards Jerusalem, to which I have referred in my first paragraph. The station at Deir el Belah, where the headquarters of the General Officer Commanding, Eastern Force, had been set up on 30th March, was opened on the 5th April, and was rapidly developed into an important rail-head. At this period the activity of hostile aircraft in bombing Deir el Belah and other

advanced camps considerably increased, but little damage was done, and all attacks were followed by vigorous retaliation on the part of the Royal Flying Corps. The troops were all concentrated ready for an advance and reconnaissances for artillery positions east of the Wadi Ghuzze were completed early in April, but the chief factor in fixing the date of the advance was our continual source of anxiety, the water-supply. It was necessary for the next advance that two divisions should be able to water in the Wadi Ghuzze, where the prospects of obtaining water by well-sinking were small. Tanks therefore had to be set up in the Wadi, and arrangements made to pump rail-borne water from Deir el Belah over the In Seirat ridge to fill them. These preparations were energetically put in hand, and even by the 9th April 27,000 gallons were in the cistern at Um Jerrar, and excavations for three 8,000-gallon tanks at Tel el Jemmi were completed, while nine cisterns with a total capacity of 60,000 gallons, and seven empty cisterns, were located at Abasan el Kebir.

The general plan of the attack had by this time already been decided. It was that the advance on Gaza with three infantry divisions and two cavalry divisions should take place in two stages. The first stage would be the occupation of the Sheikh Abbas—Mansura ridge, south of Gaza, and its preparation as a strong point from which any flank attack could easily be repelled. A short period of development was to follow the first stage, during which water-supply and communications would be improved as far as possible, heavy artillery and Tanks brought up and supplies advanced, so that the final stage—an advance on Gaza after a heavy bombardment—should be accomplished rapidly. Meanwhile, the enemy in front of me had been considerably reinforced, and had abandoned all intention of further retirement. It became clear that five divisions and a cavalry division had now appeared on our front, with an increase in heavy artillery. Not only were the Gaza defences being daily strengthened and wired, but a system of enemy trenches and works was being constructed south-east from Gaza to the Atawineh ridge, some 12,000 yards distant from the town. This put any encircling movement by our cavalry out of the question, unless the enemy's line in front of us could be pierced, and a passage made through which the mounted divisions could be pushed. Until that could be done, the rôle of our mounted troops would be to protect the right flank of the infantry, whose attack in the final stage was to be on the same lines as the first attack. While one division advanced from the Wadi Ghuzze between the sea and the Gaza —Deir el Belah road, the two divisions occupying the Sheikh Abbas—Mansura ridge were to attack the south-western defences up to the Ali Muntar hill; the right division, after overcoming the enemy on its front, to pivot on its left against the defences north of Ali Muntar. The 17th April was fixed as the first stage of the advance, and on the 15th April I proceeded to Khan Yunus, where I set up my Advanced General Headquarters.

10. For the first stage of the operations the dispositions of the General Officer Commanding, Eastern Force, were as follows :—The 52nd and 54th Divisions, the latter on the right, to seize and occupy the line Sheikh Abbas—Mansura—Kurd Hill (on the El Sire ridge). The General Officer Commanding, 52nd Division, Major-General W. E. B. Smith, C.B., C.M.G.,

to command this attack. The 53rd Division, under the command of Major-General S. F. Mott, to remain in position just north of the Wadi Ghuzze between the sea and the Gaza—Khan Yunus road, but to carry out strong reconnaissances northwards along the coast. The 74th Division to remain in general reserve in the vicinity of In Seirat. Of the Desert Column, now constituted of two mounted divisions and the Imperial Camel Corps Brigade, one mounted division was to be disposed about Shellal with the object of immobilising enemy forces at Hereira, while the remainder of the column was to protect the right flank of the 54th Division. The enemy was disposed in a chain of detachments along the 16 miles between Sharia and Gaza, with strong trenches at Rijm el Atawineh (about 13,000 yards south-east of Gaza) and very strong defences, known as the Warren, the Labyrinth, Green Hill, Middlesex Hill, Outpost Hill and Lees Hill (see inset, Map 4), running south-westwards along the ridge from Ali Muntar. This position, which commands all approaches to the town from the south-west, south and south-east, had been very strongly fortified and well wired, in addition to the natural obstacles formed by thick cactus hedges, and had been made into a nest of machine guns, largely manned by Germans. The right of his line, between Gaza and the sea, ran in the arc of a circle west and south-west of the town. This section consisted of a double line of trenches and redoubts, strongly held by infantry and machine guns, well placed and concealed in impenetrable cactus hedges built on high mud banks enclosing orchards and gardens on the outskirts of the town.

The advance began at dawn on 17th April, and

the Sheikh Abbas—Mansura—Kurd Hill position was taken by 7 a.m. with little opposition and practically no casualties, though one Tank was put out of action by direct hits from artillery. The consolidation of the position was at once begun under intermittent bursts of heavy shelling. The Desert Column fulfilled its task of protection and reconnaissance, during which a strong body of enemy cavalry was dislodged by a brigade of the Australian and New Zealand Mounted Division from a ridge just east of the Wadi Imleih. The mounted troops of the Desert Column fell back west of the Wadi Ghuzze for the night, leaving an outpost line from the right of the 54th Division southwards. Consolidation of the Sheikh Abbas—Mansura position continued during the night, and all other preparations for the second stage of the advance, which was ordered to take place on the 19th, were pushed on during the 18th. On this day the Desert Column again made strong reconnaissances towards the east. The Imperial Camel Corps Brigade was detached from the Desert Column and placed under the orders of the General Officer Commanding, 54th Division.

The dispositions for the final stage, in which the guns of the French battleship " Requin " and of H.M. Monitors Nos. 21 and 31 were to co-operate, were as follows :—

The 54th and 52nd Divisions, acting under the command of General Officer Commanding, 52nd Division, were to attack the Ali Muntar group of works, the 54th pivoting on the right of the 52nd, and including in its objective the group of trenches at Sihan, east of Gaza, the Imperial Camel Corps Brigade being attached to it for this purpose. The 53rd Division was to attack the enemy trenches in the sand dunes southwest of Gaza, the line Sampson Ridge—Sheikh Ajlin being its first objective.

The 74th Division, in general reserve, was to advance and take up a position of readiness behind the Sheikh Abbas and Mansura ridges. Of the Desert Column, the Imperial Mounted Division was to make a dismounted attack on the enemy's position at Rijm el Atawineh, part of the Australian and New Zealand Mounted Division to seize a spur at Baiket el Sana on the right of the Imperial Mounted Division, and the remainder to be held in reserve to take advantage of any success gained by the Imperial Mounted Division.

The containing attack by the cavalry began at dawn, and by 10.30 a.m. the Imperial Mounted Division was on the line Gaza—Baiket el Sana Ridge, with its right refused, while the Australian and New Zealand Mounted Division had seized the ridge at Baiket el Sana. The Imperial Mounted Division, under shell and machine-gun fire, continued the attack on the Atawineh trenches with the greatest gallantry, but could make little headway. For the main attack, the bombardment opened at 5.30 a.m. The guns of the "Requin" and the monitors bombarded Ali Muntar and the works immediately to the south-west. These guns kept the enemy's defences and dug-outs under an accurate and sustained fire, and were instrumental during the day in rendering several enemy counter-attacks abortive. At 7.15 a.m. the 53rd Division advanced on Sampson Ridge and Sheikh Ajlin, and at 7.30 a.m. the Imperial Camel Corps Brigade, 54th Division and 52nd Division advanced to the attack. The 53rd Division, though meeting with considerable opposition, gradually worked up to Sampson Ridge, which was carried by the 160th Brigade early in the afternoon. This enabled the 159th Brigade to carry the high ground between this position and the coast with little opposition, and the first objective of the division was attained. The remainder of the main attack was not so fortunate. The 155th Brigade, the left brigade of the 52nd Division, made good Lees Hill, the nearest point to our line of the enemy's defences on the Ali Muntar ridge, by 8.15 a.m., but on advancing beyond Lees Hill this brigade came under very heavy machine-gun fire from Outpost Hill, which checked its progress. This prevented any advance of the 156th Brigade, which was echeloned slightly in the right rear of the 155th. A little later, one of the Tanks came astride of the lunette on Outpost Hill, causing considerable loss to the enemy, but the infantry could not capture this lunette till shortly after 10 a.m. The Tank was unfortunately hit by three shells and burnt out. Meanwhile, the 54th Division, with the Imperial Camel Corps Brigade, had advanced steadily under fire on the right of the 52nd Division. Its left brigade, the 162nd, was in advance of the right of the 156th Brigade, and thus exposed to a heavy enfilade fire from the direction of Ali Muntar. At 9.30 a.m. the left of this brigade was heavily counter-attacked, but the enemy were repulsed by machine-gun fire. On the right of the 162nd Brigade, the 163rd Brigade fought its way forward against enemy works between Gaza and Sihan. One Tank advanced ahead of the infantry and inflicted heavy casualties on the enemy in a redoubt, but was afterwards hit by shell fire and burnt out. The Imperial Camel Corps Brigade, in conjunction with the 4th Australian Light Horse Brigade on its right, entered the enemy trenches at Sihan by 9 a.m., the enemy withdrawing to a position some 800 yards to the north. The Imperial Camel Corps Brigade was unable, however, to advance beyond Sihan, and the 163rd and 162nd Brigades, in spite of most strenuous and gallant efforts to advance, were repeatedly checked by very heavy fire from this front. Towards noon the left of the 163rd Brigade was forced back by a determined counter-attack from the north-east, and this left the 162nd Brigade in a critical position, but it stood firm until, assisted by the 161st Brigade, the 163rd Brigade was able to regain all the ground it had lost. The enemy counter-attack against the 163rd Brigade was meanwhile continued against the 4th Australian Light Horse Brigade, which was forced to give ground, and, with the 3rd Australian Light Horse Brigade on its right, suffered heavy casualties. However, the Imperial Camel Corps Brigade, though in a critical position, held on till the 6th Mounted Brigade filled the gap and stopped the enemy's advance. Heavy shelling and machine-gun fire were directed at the line during the remainder of the afternoon. Meanwhile the 155th Brigade was shelled out of its position on Outpost Hill, but the position was most gallantly retaken on his own initiative by Major W. T. Forrest, M.C., 1/4th Battalion King's Own Scottish Borderers (subsequently killed), who collected a few men for the purpose. All further attempts by the 155th Brigade to launch an attack from Outpost Hill were shattered by fire at their inception, and the 156th Brigade was forced to remain in the open under a heavy fire.

11. The position at 3 p.m. was therefore as follows: The operations of the Desert Column (in effect a "containing attack") were meeting with all the success

which had been anticipated. A serious enemy counter-attack had been checked and driven back.

The 54th Division, on the right of the main attack, had progressed, in spite of determined opposition and heavy casualties, as far as was possible until a further advance of the 52nd Division should prevent the exposure of its left flank. Reports received from the 54th Division stated that the situation was satisfactory, and that no help was required in order to enable the ground gained to be held until further progress by the 52nd Division should render practicable a renewal of the advance. I should like to state here my appreciation of the great skill with which General Hare handled his fine division throughout the day.

The 52nd Division was unable to advance beyond Outpost Hill. Middlesex Hill, and a large area of extremely broken ground west and north-west of it, had been made by the enemy exceedingly strong. The nests of machine guns in the broken ground could not be located among the narrow dongas, holes and fissures with which this locality was seamed. Partly owing to this, and partly owing to the extent of the area, the artillery fire concentrated upon it was unable to keep down the enemy's fire when the 155th Brigade attempted to advance. The reserve Brigade of the 52nd Division had not been employed, and the remaining brigade (the 156th) was in position ready to attack Green Hill and Ali Muntar as soon as the progress of the 155th brigade on its left should enable it to do so. Up to this time, therefore, only one brigade of the 52nd Division was seriously engaged. The conformation of the ground, however, was such that the attack on Outpost and Middlesex Hills could only be made on an extremely narrow front. It is possible that if the General

Officer Commanding, Eastern Force, had now decided to throw in his reserves, the key of the position might have been taken with the further loss of between 5,000 and 6,000 men, but this would have left my small force, already reduced, with a difficult line of front to hold against increasing reinforcements of the enemy, who, owing to the conformation of the terrain, could attack from several directions. As it was, the General Officer Commanding, Eastern Force, in view of information received that our attack had not yet succeeded in drawing in the enemy's reserves, decided that the moment had not yet come for an attempt to force a decision by throwing in the general reserve, though he moved the 229th Brigade of the 74th Division up to Mansura, so as to be ready to press home the attack of the 52nd Division whenever required.

At 3.30 p.m. an enemy counter-attack against the left of the 162nd Brigade was shattered by our shell fire with heavy loss to the enemy, but otherwise no change occurred in the situation till 6.20 p.m., when the 155th Brigade was forced to evacuate Outpost Hill. Since it was evident that the action could not be brought to a conclusion within the day, at 4 p.m. I issued, personally, instructions to General Officer Commanding, Eastern Force, that all ground gained during the day must, without fail, be held during the night, with a view to resuming the attack on the Ali Muntar position under cover of a concentrated artillery bombardment at dawn on the 20th.

The position at nightfall was that the 53rd Division held the Sampson Ridge—Sheikh Ajlin line; the 52nd Division on its right was facing north towards Outpost Hill and Ali Muntar; the 54th Division carried the line south-eastwards and southwards round the Sheikh

Abbas ridge to El Meshrefe, whence the mounted troops continued the line southwards to the Wadi Ghuzze. Our total casualties had amounted to some 7,000.

During the night of the 19th/20th I received a message from General Dobell to say that, after careful deliberation and consultation with all divisional commanders, he was strongly of the opinion that the resumption of the attack ordered for the following morning did not offer sufficient prospect of success to justify the very heavy casualties which such an operation would, in his opinion, involve. He therefore urgently requested my sanction to cancel the instructions previously issued, and my approval for the substitution of orders for the consolidation of the positions already gained, to be carried out on the 20th, with a view to a further attack on the enemy's line at some point between Gaza and Hereira, as and when an opportunity might offer. In view of the strongly-expressed opinion of the General Officer Commanding, Eastern Force, supported by the General Officer Commanding, Desert Column, and the divisional commanders, I assented to this proposal.

12. The ground gained by the end of the 19th April was consolidated during the 20th. No ground, in fact, gained on the day has since been lost, and the position to which we then advanced has facilitated, and will facilitate, further operations. The enemy, contrary to my expectations, made no general counter-attack on the 20th, and all his local counter-attacks were easily repulsed. One counter-attack was nipped in the bud entirely by our aircraft; a reconnaissance machine having detected about 2,000 infantry and 800 cavalry gathered in the Wadi near Hereira, four

machines immediately attacked this force, which they found in massed formation, with bombs, and the entire body was dispersed with heavy casualties.

On 21st April, General Dobell visited me at my Advanced General Headquarters to discuss the situation. He repeated that, in his opinion, which was confirmed by that of all his subordinate commanders, in view of the great strength of the positions to which he was opposed, the renewal of a direct attack with the force at his disposal would not be justified by any reasonable prospect of success. He was most strongly of the opinion that deliberate methods must be adopted, and that even the assumption of trench warfare might be necessary, pending the arrival of reinforcements. After full discussion, and not without considerable reluctance, I assented to this change of policy, and on the 22nd April I reported to the War Office that with my present force I could not probably count on being able to effect more than a local success.

In the meantime, it became apparent to me that General Dobell, who had suffered some weeks previously from a severe touch of the sun, was no longer in a fit state of health to bear the strain of further operations in the coming heat of summer. To my great regret, therefore, I felt it my duty to relieve him of his command, and to place the command of Eastern Force in the hands of Lieut.-General Sir Philip Chetwode, Bt., K.C.M.G., C.B., D.S.O. General Chetwode was succeeded in command of the Desert Column by Major-General Sir H. G. Chauvel, K.C.M.G., C.B.; and Major-General E. W. C. Chaytor, C.B., C.M.G., succeeded to the command of the Australian and New Zealand Mounted Division. Accordingly, on the morning of the 21st, I interviewed General Dobell and informed him of my decision, in which he concurred. I then interviewed General Chetwode, and instructed him to relieve General Dobell in the command of Eastern Force. On 26th April, I received the decision of the War Cabinet, referred to in my first paragraph, which substituted for previous instructions to advance on Jerusalem, instructions to take any favourable opportunity of defeating the Turkish forces opposed to me, and follow up any success gained with all the means at my disposal.

13. After this time no notable change took place in the situation on the eastern front, where the immediate task was so to consolidate the first line that it could be held by the minimum of troops, thus releasing one or two divisions for further offensive operations. The enemy continued to receive reinforcements for his units and additional troops, so that early in May I estimated that he had nearly six infantry divisions on his front line, while his total force in this theatre might amount to eight divisions. There was no doubt, moreover, that he had lately received considerable reinforcements in artillery and machine-gun units, as well as in mounted troops. Throughout the month he continued to strengthen his positions between Gaza and Hereira, and began to build a military branch line from El Tine, on the Central Palestine Railway, towards El Mejdel, north of Gaza.

As the result of recent operations, I was closely in touch with the enemy on a front of some 14,000 yards from Sheikh Ajlin, on the sea, to the northeastern corner of the Sheikh Abbas ridge. From that point my line turned back through Sharta towards the Wadi Ghuzze, with the right flank extended to Shellal in order to protect my southern flank and to deny to the enemy the valuable supplies lying in the Wadi at that point. In the meantime, arrangements had been made to construct a branch line of railway as rapidly as possible from Rafa to the neighbourhood of Shellal, to enable operations to be conducted on a broader front than was possible from the single rail-head at Deir el Belah. By 23rd June this branch line had progressed to the 25th kilometre, and stations had been made at Amr and Weli Sheikh Nuran. The process of strengthening the northern portion of the position, from the sea to Sharta, in order to set free as many troops as possible, was energetically continued during the month of May, by the end of which it was possible, roughly speaking, to hold this portion with two divisions, thus leaving two divisions in general reserve. The mounted troops of the Desert Column were untiring in reconnaissance towards the east and northeast during this time. For the time being, however, the possibility of offensive action was governed by the fact that, exclusive of the mounted troops, I had only three fully-equipped and trained divisions and one partially equipped and trained. The three former divisions required some 350 officers and 9,000 other ranks to bring them up to full strength. During April and May one battalion arrived from East Africa, one from Aden, and four from India towards the formation of a further division, to be called the 75th, but the health of the two former was much impaired, and on the 12th May I was informed that the remaining battalions destined for this division were to be retained in India for the present. At the same time I was informed that two mounted brigades would be sent to me from Salonica, together with complete artillery for one division, and also appreciable reinforcements in heavy

FOURTH DESPATCH 167

artillery. On 27th May I was informed that the remainder of this division, the 60th, would sail for Egypt from Salonica during June. These prospective additions to the force entailed a considerable amount of reorganisation, and at the same time it became necessary to reorganise the transport of the fighting units, in regard to which, in the exigencies of recent operations, improvisation to meet the needs of the moment had, of necessity, been resorted to.

14. From 6th May the defensive line from Sheikh Ajlin to Tel el Jemmi was reorganised into two sections, to be held on a regular system of reliefs. Cavalry patrolling was actively carried on by the mounted troops, who frequently came into contact with the enemy's mounted patrols to the east and north-east. During the earlier part of May, the enemy aircraft made several attacks with bombs on Deir el Belah and other points near the front line. The Royal Flying Corps made effective retaliation against Ramle and Sharia, and, as the month advanced, the enemy's activity diminished in this respect. During May, also, our heavy batteries, with the co-operation of the Royal Flying Corps, made very effective practice on enemy batteries in the neighbourhood of Gaza. The only event, however, of any note during this month was a cavalry raid carried out on the 23rd and 24th May against the Beersheba—El Auja railway, with the object of preventing the enemy from recovering and using its material for the construction of his branch line from El Tine to Mejdel.

The plans for this operation necessitated the movement of one mounted brigade and demolition parties to Bir el Esani, 10 miles W.S.W. of Beersheba on the Wadi Shanag, during the afternoon before the raid took place. Since this movement could not be concealed, it was arranged that an artillery demonstration should take place on the left flank, in order to draw the enemy's attention from the movement on Esani, and place him in doubt as to our intentions. For three days previously, the artillery carried out wire-cutting on the Gaza defences, and the enemy's repairing parties were kept under artillery and machine-gun fire. The artillery demonstration was made more intense during the afternoon of 22nd and the early morning of 23rd May. This demonstration was very successful in making the enemy apprehensive on his right, and he appears to have suffered a considerable number of casualties.

On the afternoon of the 22nd, one brigade of the Australian and New Zealand Mounted Division, with demolition parties from the field squadrons of both mounted divisions, moved to Esani. During the night of the 22nd/23rd this force marched on the railway at Asluj and Hadaj by way of Khalasa. Khalasa was surrounded during the night, and no opposition was met with there. The demolition parties reached their positions on the railway line just before 7 a.m. on the 23rd. The Imperial Camel Corps Brigade left Rafa early on the 22nd and marched approximately down the Turco-Egyptian frontier on Auja. Owing to the difficulties of the country, the Imperial Camel Brigade demolition party was unable to begin work on the railway before 11.45 a.m. on the 23rd. The demolition parties had previously been thoroughly trained, and their work, once begun, was carried out with great rapidity. Those of the mounted divisions completed the destruction of the railway from Asluj to Hadaj—about seven miles—by 10 a.m. The destruction of this portion of the line made interference with the work of the Imperial Camel

Brigade practically impossible. The demolition party of that brigade, therefore, had time to complete the destruction of six miles of railway eastward from Auja during the day.

Thus 13 miles of railway line were completely destroyed, each pair of rails being cut in the centre. One 6-span bridge, one 12-span bridge, a viaduct over the Wadi Theigat el Amirin, and (between Thamiliat el Rashid and Asluj) one 18-arched bridge, one 5-arched bridge, one 3-arched bridge, one 2-arched bridge, and two culverts were completely destroyed. All the points and switches at Asluj railway station were destroyed. A considerable number of telegraph posts were cut down, wires cut, and insulators broken. A quantity of Decauville material near Hadaj was destroyed. Finally, a large stone building near Wadi Imkharuba was demolished, with quantities of sandbags, timber and matting.

While this work was in progress, the mounted divisions of the Desert Column carried out a demonstration towards Bir Saba and Irgeig. The divisions marched by night on the 22nd/23rd, and during the 23rd carried a tactical and water reconnaissance of the area immediately west and north-west of Bir Saba. The 10th Heavy Battery, R.G.A., was moved forward behind this force and shelled the viaduct at Irgeig.

The withdrawal of the mounted troops was effected without difficulty, the enemy showing no signs of activity. The Australian and New Zealand Mounted Division met a few Arab snipers. One armed Arab was killed and 13 prisoners were taken. The Imperial Mounted Division encountered only slight opposition from small parties of enemy cavalry. Our casualties were one man wounded. During this operation crops which could not be brought in, and which would otherwise fall into the hands of the enemy, were destroyed by our troops. It is estimated that 120 tons were burnt during the day. One of our aeroplanes employed for intercommunication between Desert Column Headquarters and the Imperial Camel Corps Brigade was damaged in attempting to land near Auja. The Imperial Camel Corps Brigade therefore remained at that place for the night, 23rd/24th, and personnel of the brigade succeeded in repairing the aeroplane, the loss of which was thereby avoided, and which returned safely to the aerodrome on the 24th.

For the month of June there is nothing of special note to record, the period being mainly one of energetic preparation for further operations. For the time being, the infantry in the northern part of the line were confined to trench warfare, to which the troops soon adapted themselves, while to the south and south-east our cavalry patrols were daily in touch with the enemy.

15. During the period covered by this report, the situation on the western front has been such as to call for little comment. The light armoured motor batteries, light car patrols and Bikanir Camel Corps, who form the garrisons of the posts, have been able to keep the whole front free from disturbance. The route from Sollum to Siwa has now been improved, so that Siwa can be reached by car from Sollum in a single day.

In consequence of an agreement between the Government and Sayed Mohammed Idris, signed at Akrama on 15th April, I have approved certain regulations to govern trade with Arabs of the western parts through the market at Sollum, the main object being to treat Sayed Idris as liberally as circumstances will permit, while at the same time regulating the quantity of food offered for sale at Sollum, so as to render it impossible for the Senoussi to lay in reserve stocks of any appreciable magnitude. The General Officer Commanding, Coastal Section, has been instructed to co-operate with the Civil Administration in putting these regulations into force. I have also issued a new proclamation defining the western line of the Coastal Section, across which no person shall pass without special permit issued by the military authorities at Sollum, movement to or from Egypt, except through Sollum, being forbidden. With a view to preventing any disturbing effect on the local population, and also to prevent any feeling of mistrust which might arise in the mind of Sayed Idris by any action of our armed parties, I have given instructions that the latter should not operate beyond our western frontier, which, for purposes of convenience, was defined broadly as a line running north and south from Sollum to the western end of Melfa Oasis.

The attitude of the Sheikhs and inhabitants at Siwa is very friendly, and the former are co-operating loyally in carrying out all instructions received from the civil and military authorities regarding restrictions of trade, repair of road passes and the destruction of the Senoussi " Zawias," or teaching-houses.

No incident has occurred in the Southern Canal Section, the garrison of which has been considerably reduced since the beginning of the year. The extent of the Northern Canal Section increased continuously as the Eastern Force advanced, and at the beginning of May this command was reorganised as that of the General Officer Commanding, Palestine Lines of Communication Defences, with headquarters at El Arish.

This command now extends from the northern part of the Suez Canal to Khan Yunus, and includes the responsibility for the defence of almost the whole length of the military railway and pipe-lines. Except for attacks by hostile aircraft, no enemy attempts have been made against the lines of communication, but between 7th and 11th May a small force from this command, consisting of two companies Imperial Camel Corps and a field troop, made a successful expedition to El Auja, Birein and El Kossaima, for the purpose of blowing up the wells and water-supply at those places to the utmost possible extent. The force met with no opposition, captured five prisoners and completed successfully the demolitions, including that of the railway bridge north-east of El Auja.

In April, Colonel Sir Mark Sykes, Bt., joined my staff as Chief Political Officer, while forming part of a joint Anglo-French Political Mission in which M. Picot was the chief French representative. This mission proceeded to El Arish at the beginning of May and subsequently paid a visit to the Hedjaz.

I have great pleasure in recording the addition to the force under my command of a French detachment under M. le Colonel Piépape, and of an Italian detachment under Majer da Agostino. The French detachment took over the defences at Khan Yunus on 25th May, and the Italian detachment has proceeded to the Rafa defences. At the end of May I was most happy to welcome in Egypt M. le Général Bailloud, who came as inspector of French troops in Northern Africa to inspect the French detachment.

At the beginning of May it became necessary to reorganise the administrative services on the Eastern Lines of Communication, owing to the increasing size

FOURTH DESPATCH 173

of the Eastern Force. An inspector, Palestine Lines of Communication, was therefore appointed. His headquarters were established at Kantara on 2nd May, and the advantage of this appointment has been proved by the increased efficiency of the lines-of-communication services east of the canal.

16. In conclusion, I should like to place on record my appreciation of the magnificent work done by all the fighting troops before Gaza. No praise can be too high for the gallantry and steadfastness of the cavalry, infantry, artillery, Royal Flying Corps and all other units which took part in the two battles. Particular commendation is due to the infantry. The 52nd, 53rd and 54th Divisions, though actively engaged for over a year in the Sinai Peninsula, had not, since their reorganisation after the operations in the Dardanelles, been able to show how they had improved out of all knowledge in training and discipline, and in all that goes to make up an excellent fighting organisation. Under severe trial they have now given ample proof of the finest soldierly qualities. It is hardly necessary to reiterate the praises of the Australian and New Zealand mounted troops, who have always come up to their high reputation, and their comrades in the mounted yeomanry have shown themselves to be endowed with the same bravery, vigour and tenacity. The Imperial Camel Corps, manned by Australian, New Zealand and British personnel, has proved a *corps d'élite*, possessed with a quite remarkable spirit of gallantry. The distinguished service rendered by the troops from India is deserving of high commendation. Units of the Indian Regular Army, mounted and dismounted Imperial Service troops and the Bikanir Camel Corps have shown soldierly qualities in action, discipline and

endurance; and I wish to record the unfailing devotion to duty of the battalions in garrison in Egypt, and of the British West Indies Regiment. The Camel Transport Corps and the Egyptian Labour Corps—two units raised in this country—are worthy of the warmest praise for their untiring labours, under the severest conditions, in close conjunction with the fighting troops.

The health of the troops has throughout been singularly good. All branches of the medical services, under Surgeon-General J. Maher, C.B., deserve the highest commendation for their successful work at the front, on the lines of communication and in the base hospitals. The presence in the force of a number of civil medical consultants, who have so patriotically given their services, has been of the very greatest value, and they have worked in successful accord with the regular medical services of the Army. The Australian Army Medical Corps and the New Zealand Medical Corps have also been remarkable for their efficiency and unremitting devotion.

The workings of the supply and transport services have had to take into account quite abnormal conditions, both of supplies available and terrain, involving in some cases complete reorganisation of units to suit local conditions. In spite of this, the functions of these services have been discharged in a most admirable manner, and great credit is due to the Director, Brigadier-General G. F. Davies, C.M.G., and to all ranks under him.

The same local conditions above referred to have rendered the force more than usually dependent on animal transport, while operations have involved the use of important mounted forces. The remount and veterinary services have consequently held a vital place in the organisation, and they have carried out their respective tasks to my complete satisfaction.

I have, in a previous despatch, brought to notice the admirable work of the signal services, and I need only now add that this service has continued in its efficient and highly satisfactory condition. The work done by the engineer services and the works directorate deserves high commendation.

There is, perhaps, no department which has a greater influence upon the moral of an army than that of the Chaplains' Department. The thorough and self-sacrificing manner in which chaplains of all denominations, under the principal chaplain, Brigadier-General A. V. C. Hordern, C.M.G., have carried out their duties, has earned the gratitude of all ranks.

The impossibility of granting leave home on any extended scale has rendered the Army in the Field dependent on rest camps and voluntary institutions for that rest and relaxation so necessary in view of the arduous conditions of campaigning in the desert and in tropical heat. I wish to take this, my last, opportunity of expressing the thanks of the whole Field Force to those ladies and gentlemen who have done so much to obviate the deprivations imposed on it by those conditions. Especially are they due to the Church Army and the Young Men's Christian Association, whose recreation huts are provided, not only in the rest camps, but also throughout the front. It would be hard to exaggerate the value of these institutions, both in sustaining the moral and the health of the troops.

The dealing with reinforcements and material arriving from England, the transference of such large numbers of troops to other theatres of war, the keeping of records thus affected and the registration of casualties and evacuation of sick and wounded, have thrown very heavy work on the base ports. The staffs responsible for these matters have discharged their arduous duties with marked efficiency, frequently under difficult climatic conditions and abnormal pressure.

In spite of the important operations in progress during this time, military training has been continued with undiminished vigour. The Imperial School of Instruction at Zeitoun has by now passed over 22,000 officers and non-commissioned officers through its hands.

A staff school was started early in the year for the training of junior staff officers. Three courses, each of about six weeks, were held at this school, for which accommodation was found just outside Cairo, the number of candidates at the first two courses being shared between this force and the Salonica Force, while the last course was confined to the Egyptian Expeditionary Force. The results of these courses have been exceedingly useful, and the instruction has been extremely well carried out.

His Highness the Sultan has, throughout the period of my command, given me valuable encouragement and wise counsel, based on his unrivalled knowledge of Eastern affairs.

I wish once more to thank His Excellency The High Commissioner, General Sir F. R. Wingate, G.C.B., G.C.V.O., K.C.M.G., D.S.O., for the ready assistance and quick sympathy which he has given me in all my work; all branches of the Civil Government of Egypt have assisted the Forces in the Field with unfailing readiness.

My gratitude is also due to Vice-Admiral Sir

Rosslyn Wemyss, K.C.B., C.M.G., M.V.O., Commander-in-Chief, East Indies and Egypt, for his part in securing the unfailing co-operation of the Royal Navy at all times; and I wish to make special reference to the admirable and gallant work done by the Naval Air Service, which has been of the greatest assistance to my operations.

My Chief of the General Staff, Major-General Sir Arthur Lynden Lynden-Bell, K.C.M.G., C.B., has given me unvarying and loyal support at all times. He has proved himself an ideal Chief of the General Staff, combining a thorough knowledge of his duties with an activity and an energy that overcomes all difficulties. He has earned the confidence of all ranks.

Major-General John Adye, C.B., has been an excellent Deputy Adjutant-General, having great knowledge of all administrative work, and sound judgment. He has been of the greatest assistance to me.

Major-General Sir Walter Campbell, K.C.M.G., C.B., D.S.O., my Deputy Quartermaster-General, is an organiser of great general ability, very sound and hard-working. I owe a great debt of gratitude to this officer.

The General Officer Commanding, Eastern Force, Lieut.-General Sir P. W. Chetwode, Bt., K.C.M.G., C.B., D.S.O., has united the qualities of brilliant leadership and sure judgment, and has invariably inspired confidence in all ranks.

The labours of a Commander-in-Chief in the Field are considerably lightened when the complex and difficult duties which fall to the military secretary are ably discharged. In this respect I have been fortunate. Lieut.-Colonel S. H. Pollen, C.M.G., is an officer of outstanding ability and sound judgment, and the manner in which he has carried out his duties has greatly contributed to the smooth working of the staff, and is beyond praise.

I am submitting, in a further despatch, the names of officers, non-commissioned officers and men and others whom I wish to bring to notice for gallant and distinguished service during the period under review.

I have the honour to be,
Your Lordship's most obedient Servant,
(Signed) A. J. MURRAY, General,
Commander-in-Chief,
Egyptian Expeditionary Force.

APPENDICES

APPENDIX A

TABLE SHOWING UNITS EMBARKED FROM EGYPT BETWEEN JANUARY 9TH AND MAY 31ST, 1916

(a) Units other than Medical Units

Unit.	Date.	Destination.	Offcrs.	Other Ranks.	Follrs.	Anmls.	Vhcles.	Guns.	
46th Division [1]	4th Feb.–1st Mar.	Marseilles	135	2,587	—	82	258	—	
13th Division	5th Feb.–20th Apl.	Basrah	806	22,183	—	10,298	2,541	72	
15th Sikhs	14th February	Bombay	22	464	77	84	—	2	
1/5th Gurkhas	14th and 28th Feb.	Bombay	26	639	51	64	—	2	
1/6th Gurkhas	14th–17th Feb.	Bombay	23	613	30	20	—	3	
2/8th Gurkhas	15th February	Bombay	23	531	79	85	—	2	
1/4th Gurkhas	15th February	Bombay	30	715	56	53	—	—	
2/2nd Gurkhas	17th February	Bombay	30	889	71	85	—	2	
33rd Punjabis	16th February	Aden	34	898	82	85	—	4	
No. 7 Brigade Indian Mountain Artillery	21st and 22nd Feb.	Basrah	18	851	—	541	84	12	
254th Tunnelling Co., R.E.	24th February	Marseilles	12	85	—	—	—	—	
31st Division	28th Feb.–28th Mar.	Marseilles	659	18,441	—	2,618	292	79	284 cycles
39th Garwhals	28th February	India	36	1,315	93	80	—	—	
1st Indian Labour Corps	1st March	Basrah	15	967	62	—	—	—	
108th Indian Fd. Amb.	1st March	Basrah	11	11	149	—	—	—	
29th Division	2nd Mar.–18th Apl.	Marseilles	719	18,395	—	3,762	300	90	
R.M.A. Special Heavy Detachment	8th March	Marseilles	6	70	—	—	16	1	5 tractors 1 lorry
2nd Australian Division	14th Mar.–21st May	Marseilles	757	21,980	—	3,415	446	32	

APPENDIX A

Unit	Date	Port							Notes
1st Australian Division	20th Mar.–30th May	Marseilles	796	24,155	—	4,461	—	—	
24th Labour Co., A.S.C.	26th March	Marseilles	4	392	—	—	—	—	
18th Labour Co., A.S.C.	26th March	Marseilles	5	309	—	—	—	—	
27th Labour Co., A.S.C.	26th March	Marseilles	2	366	—	—	—	—	
1st Anzac Headquarters	30th Mar. & 7th Apl.	Marseilles	26	156	—	45	—	—	
15th Mule Corps	4th April	Basrah	1	376	—	581	—	—	
1st Mule Corps	4th April	Basrah	—	126	—	109	—	—	
New Zealand Division	7th Apl.–30th May	Marseilles	808	21,386	—	3,756	112	34	4 tractors
Heavy Artillery Units	9th and 15th April	Marseilles	84	2,285	—[1]	129	—	—	25 lorries
South African Brigade	13th Apl.–8th May	Marseilles	161	4,389	—	64	—	—	
1st City of Edinburgh Co., R.E.	15th–18th April	Marseilles	6	243	—	8	21	—	
1st Renfrew Co., R.E.	15th and 18th April	Marseilles	6	231	—	8	21	—	
167th Co., R.E.	15th April	Marseilles	3	139	—	3	11	—	
London Brigade	15th Apl.–8th May	Marseilles	104	1,961	—	30	—	—	
133rd A.T. Co., R.E.	15th April	Marseilles	3	101	—	—	8	—	
134th A.T. Co., R.E.	15th April	Marseilles	3	110	—	—	8	—	
136th A.T. Co., R.E.	15th April	Marseilles	1	128	—	—	3	—	
Mining Corps, A.I.F.	27th April	Marseilles	52	1,147	—	—	—	—	
Stokes Batteries	3rd May	Basrah	24	276	—	—	—	48	1 car
Patiala Lancers	7th May	Aden	33	726	—	837	—	—	
2/7th Middlesex	9th May	Marseilles	28	890	—	—	—	—	
2/8th Middlesex	9th May	Marseilles	27	822	—	—	—	—	
1/6th Royal Scots	9th May	Marseilles	32	931	—	—	—	—	
2/10th Gurkha Rifles	10th and 13th May	Aden	27	779	—	138	—	4	
14th K.G.O. Sikhs	10th May	Aden	27	720	—	140	—	4	
105th Indian Field Amb.	10th May	Aden	5	188	—	27	—	—	
2nd Gn. Bn. Liverpool Rgt.	11th May	Mudros	27	906	—	6	—	—	
W. Lancs. Field Co., R.E.	11th May	Mudros	5	210	—	77	18	—	
TOTAL			**5,662**	**156,082**	**750**	**31,691**	**4,139**	**391**	

[1] A small portion of this division, originally intended for defence of the Canal, had already arrived in Egypt when it was decided that it should remain in France.

(b) MEDICAL UNITS

Unit.	Date.	Destination.	Numbers.			
			Officers.	Other Ranks.	Nurses.	
23rd Stationary Hospital	18th February	Basrah	14	119	27	From U.K. and transhipped.
No. 16 Casualty Clearing Station	February	Basrah	8	84	—	
108th Indian Field Ambulance	February	Basrah	10	168	—	
135th Indian Field Ambulance	February	Basrah	14	173	—	
137th (D Sect.) Indian Field Ambulance	February	Basrah	4	51	—	
No. 5 Indian Departmental Medical Stores	February	Basrah	1	4	—	
No. 19 Stationary Hospital	27th February	East Africa	16	122	27	
No. 1 Canadian Stationary Hospital	28th February	Salonica	16	124	29	From U.K. and transhipped
"Y" Indian General Hospital	4th March	Bombay	11	184	—	
"Z" Indian General Hospital	11th March	Bombay	10	205	—	From U.K. and transhipped
No. 32 General Hospital	22nd March	Basrah	34	271	73	
No. 32 General Hospital (Advance Party)	22nd March	Basrah	2	3	—	
No. 3 Canadian Stationary Hospital	24th March	United Kingdom	16	124	29	
No. 2 Australian General Hospital	26th March	France	22	185	115	

APPENDIX A

No. 1 Australian General Hospital	29th March	France	25	188	115	From France and transhipped
Bombay Presidency General Hospital	5th April	Bombay	13	209	6	
Lahore Stationary Hospital	10th April	Bombay	10	114	—	From France and transhipped
Meerut X-Ray Section	10th April	Bombay	1	3	—	
No. 7 Canadian General Hospital	11th April	United Kingdom	15	119	25	
No. 2 Australian Casualty Clearing Station	21st April	France	12	85	—	
No. 11 Casualty Clearing Station	21st April	France	8	79	—	
No. 35 Casualty Clearing Station	21st April	France	9	77	—	
No. 15 Stationary Hospital	22nd April	East Africa	16	126	27	
No. 14 Casualty Clearing Station	22nd April	East Africa	11	84	—	
No. 52 Casualty Clearing Station	22nd April	East Africa	11	80	—	
No. 19 Motor Ambulance Convoy	22nd April	East Africa	7	141	—	
No. 8 Indian General Hospital	26th April	Bombay	9	169	—	From U.K. and transhipped
No. 17 Stationary Hospital	26th April	Bombay	16	122	27	
No. 16 Stationary Hospital	2nd May	Bombay	13	122	16	
No. 22 Stationary Hospital	10th May	Bombay	13	118	27	
No. 33 General Hospital	24th May	Bombay	35	190	73	From U.K. and transhipped
No. 8A Indian General Hospital	23rd February	Bombay	12	147	—	From U.K. and transhipped
No. 1 Indian General Hospital	25th February	Bombay	13	184	—	From U.K. and transhipped
		TOTAL	427	4,174	616	

APPENDIX B

SHOWING THE CHIEF COMBATANT UNITS OF THE MEDITERRANEAN EXPEDITIONARY FORCE IN EGYPT ON 27TH JANUARY, 1916

General Headquarters Troops :—
    Bikanir Camel Corps.
    5th Wing, Royal Flying Corps.
    20th Brigade, R.G.A. (3 batteries of 4 60-pounders).
    35th Brigade, R.G.A. (3 batteries of 4 60-pounders).
    24th Brigade, R.G.A. (1 battery of 4 6-in. howitzers).
                            (1 battery of 2 9.2-in. howitzers).
                            (1 section of 2 6-in. Mark VII guns).
    32nd Brigade, R.G.A. (2 batteries of 4 6-in. howitzers).
    14th Siege Battery, R.G.A. (4 6-in. howitzers).
    48th Siege Battery, R.G.A. (4 9.2-in. howitzers).
    4th Highland Mounted Brigade, R.G.A. (T.F.) (8 2.75-in. guns).
    2 Armoured Motor Batteries.

9th Army Corps (No. 1 Section) :—
    11th Division.
    29th Division.
    42nd Division.
    10th Indian Division.

    Corps Troops. 4th (now 8th) Mounted Brigade.
                       2nd and 3rd Dismounted Brigades.

Australian and New Zealand Army Corps (No. 2 Section) :—
    1st Australian Division.
    2nd Australian Division.
    New Zealand and Australian Division.

    Corps Troops. Australian and New Zealand Mounted Division (less 1 brigade lent to the Force in Egypt).

APPENDIX B

15th Army Corps (No. 3 Section) :—
    13th Division.
    31st Division.
    52nd Division.

    Corps Troops. 1st (now 5th) Mounted Brigade.
                       1st Dismounted Brigade.

Lines of Communication Defence Troops :—
    Imperial Service Cavalry Brigade.
    3 Garrison Battalions.

NOTE

The chief troops then composing the Force in Egypt were as follows :—
    2nd (now 6th) Mounted Brigade.
    1/1st North Midland (now 22nd) Mounted Brigade.
    Imperial Yeomanry Brigade (2 regiments).
    53rd Division.
    54th Division.
    2/1st London Infantry Brigade.
    Composite Territorial Infantry Brigade.
    South African Infantry Brigade (subsequently).
    15th (Ludhiana) Sikhs.
    " A " Battery, H.A.C.
    Notts. and Berks. Batteries, R.H.A. (T.F.).
    Coast Defence Artillery.
    Hong Kong and Singapore Mountain Battery (6 10-pounders).
    2 Armoured Trains.
    Garrison Battalions.
    Motor Machine-Gun Battery.
    Naval Armoured Cars.

APPENDIX C

SHOWING THE CHIEF COMBATANT UNITS OF THE EGYPTIAN EXPEDITIONARY FORCE IN MAY, 1916, AFTER THE DEPARTURE OF 6 DIVISIONS AND OTHER SMALLER UNITS

General Headquarters Troops :—
   Imperial Camel Corps.
   Bikanir Camel Corps.
   5th Wing, Royal Flying Corps.
   20th Brigade, R.G.A. (3 batteries of 4 60-pounders).
   Stokes Gun Batteries of 4 Infantry Brigades.
   2 Anti-aircraft Sections (each 2 13-pounders).
   4th Highland Mounted Brigade, R.G.A. (T.F.) (8 2.75-in. guns).
   Coast Defence Artillery.

No. 1 Section, Eastern Force :—
   42nd Division (with 3rd Dismounted Brigade attached).
   54th Division.
   7 Battalions Indian Infantry (one at Tor and Abu Zeneima).
   Mounted Troops. 8th Mounted Brigade.

No. 2 Section, Eastern Force (2nd Australian and New Zealand Army Corps) :—
   4th Australian Division.
   5th Australian Division.
   Mounted Troops. Australian and New Zealand Mounted Division (less 3 brigades).

No. 3 Section, Eastern Force :—
   52nd Division (with 1st Dismounted Brigade attached).
   11th Division (in reserve).
   Mounted Troops. 5th Mounted Brigade.
         Australian and New Zealand Mounted Division (less 1 brigade).

APPENDIX C

Western Frontier Force (including North-Western and South-Western Forces) :—
  53rd Division (with 4th Dismounted Brigade attached).
  2nd Dismounted Brigade.
  3 Battalions West Indies Regiment.
  Mounted Troops. 6th Mounted Brigade (with 1/2nd Co. of London Yeomanry attached).
  22nd Mounted Brigade.
  Notts. and Berks. Batteries, R.H.A. (T.F.).
  Hong Kong and Singapore Mountain Battery.
  4 Armoured Motor Batteries.
  2 Armoured Trains.

Lines of Communication Defence Troops :—
  Imperial Service Cavalry Brigade (less 1 regiment).
  Garrison Battalions.

APPENDIX D

WATER-SUPPLY EAST OF THE SUEZ CANAL

From January, 1916, to June, 1917

WHEN it was decided that the construction of a defensive line east of the Suez Canal should be taken up seriously, the important question of how the troops could be provided with an adequate supply of pure water was at once considered.

No known source of fresh water existed for many miles eastward of the Canal line. Up to November, 1915, the small garrisons and posts stationed on the east bank had been supplied with water by means of water-barges from Port Said, Ismailia and Tewfik; but it was obviously impossible to employ these means on so large a scale as the new system of defences indicated.

If, by sinking deep tube-wells on the spot, drinkable water in sufficient quantity were obtainable, this was obviously the simplest and most economical plan. It was decided, therefore, after consultation with the Egyptian Geological Department, to make experimental borings at various selected points east of the Canal. Nothing, however, but salt water was obtained, although the wells were sunk to a depth of 300 feet. Later, similar borings were made in the Romani—Mahemdia region with a like result.

The only other possible source of supply was the Sweetwater Canal, which runs, roughly, parallel with, and contiguous to, the Ship Canal on its western side throughout practically its entire length. But before this supply could be utilised for the camps and defence works which were to be established eastward, it would be necessary to filter the water, as well as to get it across the Suez Canal.

Ten concentration points were selected at intervals throughout the length of the Suez Canal; and at six of these points,

APPENDIX D

viz.: Kantara, Ballah, El Ferdan, Serapeum, Shallufa and El Kubri, filtering plant has been installed. The filters are close to the Sweet-water Canal, except at El Ferdan and Ballah, where special water conduits, four miles long, have had to be excavated.

Of the other four selected points, Ferry Post has received its water, already filtered, from Ismailia town supply; El Shatt has been connected upon the eastward side with the El Kubri system, while both Kabrit and Quarantine are supplied by water-barges, the latter having a salt-water condensing plant as a stand-by.

From the filters at the six points first mentioned the purified water is carried by syphon-pipes across the bed of the Suez Canal into reinforced concrete reservoirs on the east bank.

Near these reservoirs machinery has been installed, and the water pumped forward to the camps and defences through a system of pipe-lines. This pumping-machinery had to be ordered to meet requirements, which it was impossible to forecast adequately, and the plant was therefore not always equal to the task allotted to it.

When preparing the original scheme of water-supply it was estimated that it would be necessary to pump water to an elevation of about 200 feet. In some cases, however, posts have been established at considerably greater heights, even up to 450 feet above sea-level. To meet this difficulty, intermediate reservoirs and relay pumping stations have been provided on the pipe-lines.

Instructions to prepare for an advance in force from Romani to El Arish were issued in July. It was decided to lay down a pipe-line of 12 inches diameter to supply water for the troops and railway, and orders for the necessary material were at once placed in England.

Steps were taken to provide at Kantara an additional filter-plant capable of dealing with 500,000 gallons a day, three more 6-inch syphons under the Canal, two 250,000-gallon reservoirs, two sets of pumping engines, each of 66 h.p., in separate engine houses, to drive the water to Romani, and a special wharf to discharge machinery and pipes from ocean steamers.

The first shipload of pipes for this new main reached Kantara on the 20th September, and filtered water was flowing through the new main into reservoirs at Romani 25 miles away on the 17th November.

At Romani, at Bir el Abd, and at Mazar, in succession, storage reservoirs and pumping stations similar to those at Kantara have been provided. At the last two places construction commenced as soon as the advancing troops had secured the situation. Filtered water reached Bir el Abd, 47 miles from Kantara, on the 1st December, 1916, and it reached Mazar, 70 miles from Kantara, on the 10th January, 1917.

The pipes necessary to complete the last section of the line into El Arish reached Kantara on the 30th December, 1916, and the pipe-line into El Arish was completed by 5th February, 1917.

With the completion of the pipe-line into El Arish, the available stock of piping of over 6 inches diameter, and also of heavy engines and pipes, had been wholly absorbed. When, therefore, it was decided, in the middle of February, to extend the piped water-system east of El Arish, through Sheikh Zowaid to Rafa, it became necessary to supply the additional piping required for this extension by the collection of all available 6-inch, 5-inch, and 4-inch pipes from lines in rear, the maintenance of which was no longer essential.

This line has now been still further extended to the Wadi Ghuzze in the neighbourhood of Abu Bakra, to which point it is possible to supply by pump from Rafa up to 60,000 gallons a day.

As regards the development of local water resources in the immediate area of our present operations, there are at Khan Yunus three stone-lined wells, producing an average daily supply of from 100,000 to 120,000 gallons of good water. Pumping plant has been installed, and the greater part of this water (approximately 80,000 gallons per diem) is now distributed by pipe-line to the troops in the neighbourhood of Abasan el Kebir and Abu Sitta.

At Deir el Belah wells exist, but the water is brackish, and is not at present fit for consumption by white troops, who have therefore to be supplied with drinking-water by rail from El Arish, the local supply being utilised exclusively for watering animals. There are, however, indications that a supply of drinking-water might be developed at a lower level in this

APPENDIX D

neighbourhood by deep boring, work upon which is at present in progress in the Mendur—Jemmi area.

On the main line at present occupied by our troops in front of the Wadi Ghuzze, arrangements for supply and distribution of water are, briefly, as follows :—

Near the mouth of the Wadi, water has been developed in shallow wells in the sand dunes in sufficient quantity to supply approximately two divisions.

In the Sheikh Abbas section it has not yet been found possible to develop any local supply, and the troops are supplied with water rail-borne from El Arish, pumped forward through a pipe-line from temporary reservoirs at rail-head (Deir el Belah).

Arrangements are now well in hand to supply troops in the Mendur area with water pumped from Kantara along the pipe-line, *via* Rafa, Abu Katli, Abu Sitta and Abu Bakra. The Khan Yunus supply can also be pumped into this pipe-line.

At Shellal, springs which now produce a supply of about 200,000 gallons a day have been developed, a reservoir has been constructed to store water, and preparations are being made to install a pumping station to pump water forward in the direction of Abu Hereira.

At El Gamli and at Bir el Esani there are springs believed to be capable of extensive development, but these have not yet been fully reported on.

During the advance of the troops through the desert it was not always possible to provide a piped supply of water. It has been carried forward many miles in fantasses by camels, and in water-tanks by the railway line.

Sidings have been specially laid where trains of water-tanks on railway trucks were filled from batteries of stand-pipes. At the rail-head, at block-houses and intermediate posts, permanent reservoirs have been built or temporary canvas tanks installed.

The R.E. field companies and field squadrons on the eastern front have, provisionally, been specially organised and provided with equipment to enable them to develop local resources to the fullest possible extent. Each field company equipped for desert warfare carries 12 complete sets of pumps, water-troughs, tube wells and linings for shallow wells.

At Mahemdia, on the Mediterranean coast, and at Quarantine Station in the Gulf of Suez, condensing machinery has been erected, and is available for use in the event of failure of supplies by water-boat or other sources.

With regard to the system of filtration adopted :—

After careful consideration of the subject and consultation with engineering authorities in Egypt, it was decided that the method of mechanical purification by filters, as used in Cairo, Alexandria and other large Egyptian towns, should be employed ; and the results have been most satisfactory.

At Moascar Camp near Ismailia a slow sand-filter was installed, and has proved very successful.

APPENDIX E

RAILWAYS

From January, 1916, to June, 1917

A.—*Suez Canal Defences*

As it had been decided to increase the force in Egypt and to adopt a line of defence in front of the Suez Canal, a considerable amount of railway had to be laid. The general idea was to have nine depôts on the east bank of the Suez Canal and to have a 2-foot 6-inch gauge railway and a road from each depôt to the second line of trenches, and a 60-centimetre gauge Decauville line and a road from each depôt to the front line of trenches.

From a railway-traffic point of view it might have been better to have had two long loop lines, one south and one north of the Bitter Lakes, and one spur line from Port Said east to Mahemdia, but tactical considerations outweighed the question of convenience in railway working, and short spur lines were laid. The depôts on the east bank of the Suez Canal were to be connected with the State Railway line by swing bridges over the Suez Canal, and branch lines from the Suez Canal west bank to the State Railways' main line, whenever the distance rendered such branches advisable; the State Railway line between Port Said and Suez runs more or less parallel to the Suez Canal and west of it.

Orders were received by the State Railways to prepare a general scheme on these lines on the 25th November, 1915.

It was evident that, in order to deal with the proposed numbers of troops, the line from Zagazig to Ismailia would have to be doubled. On the 27th, 28th, 29th and 30th November, 1915, the general manager went over the ground with the General Officer in charge of the defence, and arranged to carry out his orders. Work began on the 1st December, 1915, and it was to be finished by 15th January, 1916.

The following work had to be done :—

1. *Zagazig—Ismailia Doubling.*—Line from Zagazig to Ismailia had to be doubled.

2. *Sidings from State Railways to Suez Canal.*—Sidings had to be laid from the Port Said—Suez branch of the State Railways to the Suez Canal west bank at El Ferdan, Ismailia (Ferry Post), Serapeum, Shallufa and Kubri.

3. *Stations for camps on State Railways.*—Special stations and sidings for camps were required at Ballah, Ain Ghosein, Abu Sultan, Abu Halab, Kantara, Ismailia and Suez. Large stations had already been made at Moascar and Tel el Kebir.

4. *Extra Crossing Stations on State Railways.*—Besides the special stations and sidings for camps, extra stations for crossing trains were wanted at El Hersh, Fanara and El Gebel.

In carrying out items 1, 2, 3 and 4, 150 kilometres of new standard gauge track belonging to the Egyptian State Railways were used, this being the quantity bought for doing renewals for the two years 1916–1917. All renewals have accordingly been postponed as far as the State Railways are concerned.

5. *Light Railways east of the Suez Canal.*—These lines were 2.6-inch gauge, except the one at Kantara, which was metre gauge.

6. *Standard Gauge east of Suez Canal.*—A standard $4.8\frac{1}{2}$-inch gauge line from Kantara was decided on in February, 1916, the original destination being a point in the neighbourhood of Katia.

7. *Metre Gauge and Decauville Lines.*—The metre gauge line east of Kantara, which went as far as Romani and had a branch to Dueidar, and the Decauville lines, were all laid by the Engineer-in-Chief.

The metre gauge line has been closed, and, as the material is only hired, it will be pulled up and returned to the owners.

APPENDIX E 195

B.—*Western Frontier Defences*

1. *Alexandria—Dhabba Line.*—In addition to the works for the defence of the Suez Canal, it was decided to enlarge the stations on this line in order to deal with the troops of the Western Frontier Force.

2. *Baharia Line.*—It was decided to lay a 2-foot 6-inch gauge railway from Samalut westwards for 134 kilometres in the direction of the Baharia oasis.

3. *Extension west of Kharga Oasis.*—The 2-foot 6-inch gauge line from the Nile Valley to Kharga Oasis was extended to a point 30 kilometres west of Kharga Oasis.

Item No. 1

Ismailia—Zagazig Doubling.—The doubling of this section began on the 6th December, 1915, and was completed on 6th January, 1916. It is 79 kilometres long; 15,000 men were employed on the work. The new line was laid with Egyptian Railways' standard track, which has 47-kilogram rails. Some ridges had to be widened, and, of course, stations and signalling had to be altered to suit double-line working.

Item No. 2

Sidings from State Railway between Port Said and Suez to west bank of Suez Canal.—These were laid at the following places:—

(a) *El Ferdan.*—Siding about $1\frac{1}{2}$ kilometres, with sidings for supply depôt, etc., at the end.

(b) *Ismailia.*—Siding about $2\frac{1}{2}$ kilometres long, from main line to west bank of Suez Canal at a place called Ferry Post. At Ferry Post there are railway workshops for all the 2-foot 6-inch gauge lines east of the Canal, and supply, ordnance and Royal Engineer depôts.

(c) *Serapeum.*—Siding about 3 kilometres long, with opening bridge over the Sweet-water Canal, and sidings for supplies, ordnance and Royal Engineer stores on the Suez Canal bank.

(d) *Shallufa.*— Siding 3 kilometres long, with opening bridge over Sweet-water Canal, and sidings for supplies, ordnance and Royal Engineer stores on the Suez Canal bank.

(e) *El Kubri.*—Siding 3½ kilometres long, with opening bridge over the Sweet-water Canal, and sidings for supplies, ordnance and Royal Engineer stores on the Suez Canal bank.

Item No. 3

The existing stations at the following places had to be provided with extra siding accommodation, platforms, etc. :—

(a) *El Hersh.*—New loop and platform.

(b) *Kantara.*—Very large alterations, partly owing to the necessity of providing for the traffic going from the west to the east of the Canal, partly owing to the new line from Salihiya, which was constructed in 1916. For many trains Kantara became a terminal station, so a triangle had to be provided for turning engines, and extra sidings for remarshalling trains were wanted. Platform accommodation had to be largely increased, and sidings for hospital trains and disinfecting plants had to be laid.

(c) *Ballah.*—Loop and sidings with new platform, to facilitate work on troop trains.

(d) *El Ferdan.*—Extra siding in old station, to work with siding to Canal bank mentioned in Item 2 (a) above.

(e) *Ismailia.*—New sidings in old station and three new sidings for a new goods station for army traffic, two new sidings for emergency trains to stand on.

(f) *Ain Ghosein.*—New station for cavalry camp. Two loops, siding for water train, and platform.

(g) *Serapeum.*—New station on main line for camp and for working siding mentioned above, Item 2 (c).

(h) *Abu Sultan.*—New station for camp. Two loops, water, train siding and platform.

(i) *Abu Halab.*—New station for camp. Two loops, water, train siding and platform.

APPENDIX E

(j) *Shallufa.*—New station on main line for camp and for working siding mentioned in Item 2 (d) above.

(k) *El Kubri.*—New station on main line (two loops and water siding) for camp and to work with siding referred to above, Item 2 (e).

(l)—(i.) *Suez. Camp Station.*—A new station at the north end of Suez, with siding 2 kilometres long and two loops at the end of it, for dealing with supplies, etc.

(ii.) *Suez Docks.*—The railway accommodation was insufficient here, and some new sidings were laid in; but there was very little room for sidings, and, until more land has been reclaimed, the quay lines will always be very cramped.

(m) Loops for crossing trains were put in at Fanara and El Gebel. These were for convenience in working the traffic.

Item No. 4

Details of 2-foot 6-inch gauge lines.—The material used was mainly 25-lb. rails and steel sleepers provided by the War Office. The engines were petrol-driven and gave a great deal of trouble at first. The wagons were good as regards under-frames, but the truck platforms were too narrow, and chilled cast wheels are not the best type for work in the desert. The lines were, of course, not designed for the use to which they were put. Some of the lines were laid with heavier rails and wood sleepers from the Egyptian State Railways. At first six branches were decided on, but later one was added from Port Said east to Mahemdia, and the line from Shatt to Quarantine was extended to Ayun Musa.

The lines eventually laid are as follows :—

	Length in Kilometres.
Port Said, east, to Mahemdia	41
Ballah, eastwards	8.8
El Ferdan, eastwards	9.8
Ismailia (Ferry Post), eastwards	11.3
Serapeum, eastwards	9.4
Shallufa, eastwards	15.1
El Kubri, eastwards	7.4
El Shatt to Gebel Mur	7.3
El Shatt to Ayun Musa	11.4
	121.5

A total of 121.5 kilometres, exclusive of sidings.

The first of these lines was commenced in December, 1915, and the last was completed in June, 1916, with the exception of the extension of the El Shatt line to Ayun Musa, which was decided on and completed in August.

These lines were equipped with 33 petrol locomotives and 341 trucks. The traffic varied considerably from time to time, a large part thereof consisting of stone for road-making.

The greatest tonnage on any one line in a week amounted in the case of the Shallufa line in May, 1916, to 2,900 tons, of which 2,100 tons were stone.

The weekly average tonnage carried on all the 2-foot 6-inch gauge lines in January, 1917, was 6,500 tons.

The maximum train load varied on the different lines, according to their ruling gradient, between eight and eighteen 5-ton trucks or the equivalent thereof.

These lines have all been closed, but have been left in such a condition that they can be reopened if necessary.

Item No. 5

Standard Gauge Lines east of the Suez Canal.—The standard (4-foot 8½-inch) gauge line from Kantara eastwards was commenced towards the end of February, 1916, the original destination being the neighbourhood of Katia, the materials used being 75-lb. Vignolles section steel rails on wooden sleepers with bearing plates and spikes.

Siding accommodation for locomotives and trucks was laid down at Kantara, proportional to this length of line. It has had to be largely increased subsequently, owing to the extension of the line to El Arish.

The line reached Romani (Kilometre 40.5) on the 15th May, 1916, when a branch line to Mahemdia (5½ kilometres) was taken in hand and completed on the 20th June, 1916.

The extension of the line beyond Romani began again on the 7th July, 1916, but was stopped at Kilometre 47 on the 18th July and was not resumed till the 10th August. During the intervals, much work was done in providing additional siding accommodation at Kantara and elsewhere.

APPENDIX E

The line reached Bir el Abd (Kilometre 76) on the 5th October, 1916, from which point arrangements were made for an increased rate of progress.

Bir el Mazar (Kilometre 113.5) was reached on the 17th November, 1916, and rail-head on the 16th February, 1917, was at Kilometre 170, or 15 kilometres east of El Arish.

During this period the depôt at Kantara was further enlarged and to some extent rearranged, to cope with increased traffic and the greater length of line served.

From the 16th February, 1917 (Kilometre 170), to the 28th March, 1917, when Kilometre 215 was reached, construction continued regularly, stations being laid in at El Burj, Sheikh Zowaid, Rafa and Khan Yunus—besides some smaller crossing stations necessary for traffic working.

At Kilometre 215 there was a slight check due to military operations, but work was soon resumed and rail-head reached Deir el Belah on the 4th April, 1917. Here a siding had to be laid down to the beach, four kilometres away; also a long siding (about three kilometres) for watering a post; besides the usual station with siding for supplies, hospital, etc.

The mileage of track laid in this railway is greater than might be supposed, because every alternate station has to be large enough to deal with the traffic necessary for feeding, munitioning and, to a certain extent, watering the Force.

On the 23rd April, 1917, orders were given for the construction of a branch line from Rafa to Weli Sheikh Nuran, and from there southwards to Gamli. Sheikh Nuran Station was reached on the 18th May, 1917, Gamli (Kilometre 26 from Rafa) on the 13th June, 1917.

A branch line to Shellal was started from Kilometre $22\frac{3}{4}$ on the Rafa—Gamli branch.

The large Wadi at Shellal was reached on the 15th June, 1917, and bank parties are now doing the heavy earthwork necessary to get the line down into the bed of the Wadi, across it and up the other side. There is a very large cube of earthwork here, and a bridge is wanted over the Wadi itself. The whole work is estimated to require 40 days from 3rd June, if no very hard soil or rock is met with.

Meanwhile, the track-laying parties are occupied in laying in loops for the extra crossing stations and diversions referred to above.

On the 9th March, 1917, at a conference with the Commander-in-Chief, it was settled to keep the line beyond Gaza near the coast and not to try for an inland route.

On the 10th March, 1917, a bad sand-storm began, which lasted for six days and interfered with traffic very much. It was impossible to see far, and the line became covered with sand in many places. An attempt to push traffic in spite of the storm led to six derailments in one day. It took some time to catch up the arrears of traffic. Fortunately, since then there have only been two bad days.

A steel girder bridge on cylinders is being built across Wadi el Arish and should be finished before the next rainy season; another minor bridge is being built. So far there have not been many water-courses to cross, but as the line goes north the climate changes, more rain falls, and a number of culverts will be required, besides a few larger bridges. Provision has been made for these, and the girders for the next section of the line are in the country. Rails, fish-plates and a large proportion of the sleepers have been supplied from India. The finish of the rails is equal to the best English work. It remains to be seen how they will wear.

For various reasons (mainly water and the necessity of laying large stations at frequent intervals) the capacity of the line was put at 13 trains a day on an average. This, of course, means that more than that number have to be run occasionally. The coastwise water transport has helped very much, and so far the 13 trains have seldom been needed.

A few more crossing stations have been put in, and some other alterations made, which will bring the capacity of the single line up to 16 trains each way daily on an average. If more than these are needed the water-supply must somehow be increased, and it would be wise to double the line as far as Rafa at all events, and several other points will need attention.

More rolling stock and engines have been sent from the Egyptian State Railways; 14 more South-Western locomotives and 6 more coaches have been received from England.

APPENDIX E

The total engines and vehicles now on the Kantara East line are as follows:—

	Supplied by War Office.	Supplied by Egyptian State Railways.	Total.
Engines—			
London and South-Western 0—6—0	26	—	26
Petrol	3	—	3
Egyptian State Railway 0—6—0	—	28	28
Egyptian State Railway 4—4—0	—	3	3
Egyptian State Railway 2—6—0	—	20	20
Egyptian State Railway, Tanks 0—6—0	—	2	2
Total	29	53	82
Coaches—			
4-wheeled	—	28	28
6-wheeled	—	35	35
8-wheeled	12	—	12
Total	12	63	75
Wagons—			
8, 10 and 12 tons	450	729	1,179
15 tons	—	40	40
30 tons	—	79	79
Brake vans	12	24	36
Sundry	—	26	26
Total	462	898	1,360

Traffic.—The line now carries on an average 22,890 tons a week, and has an engine mileage of 28,150 per week.

The maximum train-load is from 30 to 35 12-ton trucks, according to the class of engine employed.

Water.—Water-supply has been one of the chief difficulties to contend with, water having to be carried by rail beyond the furthest point of supply by pipe-line, to some considerable extent.

Communication with West Bank of Suez Canal.—A ferry

has been constructed at Kantara which is capable of carrying an engine (or four wagons), so that any engine or wagon which requires heavy repairs can be ferried over the Suez Canal and run up to the State Railway shops in Cairo.

B.—WESTERN FRONTIER DEFENCES

Item No. 1.—Western Frontier Force

Alexandria—Dhabba Line.—The stations on this line had to have all the crossing loops lengthened to take larger trains than the line was designed for. Full-sized trains cannot be used on this line, as the bridge over the channel from Lake Mareotis will not carry the heaviest engines.

Water.—The great difficulty on this line is water. There is none fit for troops or boilers, and all water has to be carried in tank trucks.

Rolling Stock.—Provided from Egyptian State Railway stock.

The 4-foot $8\frac{1}{2}$-inch gauge line from Alexandria to Dhabba is now working on a peace basis again. One hundred and sixty-six kilometres of good rails could be obtained from this line, if necessary, for use elsewhere, but a large number of the sleepers would need replacing, and a considerable percentage of new fastenings would be required.

Item No. 2.—Western Frontier Force

Baharia Military Railway.—The line from Samalut towards the oasis of Baharia is 134 kilometres long.

Gauge.—2 feet 6 inches.

Materials.—Steel rails, wooden sleepers, spikes, no bearing plates. Material all second-hand, bought from various light railway companies in Egypt or provided by the State Railways.

Gradient.—The ruling gradient is 1 in 100.

Traffic.—Traffic for this line goes by the State Railways' main Upper Egypt line to Maghagha, then over the Upper Egypt Auxiliary Railways to Samalut, where it is transhipped to

APPENDIX E

the 2-foot 6-inch wagons of the Baharia military line. The Upper Egypt Auxiliary Railways are light 4-foot 8½-inch gauge lines, the property of the Egyptian State Railways.

Bridges.—A large bridge had to be built over the Bahr Yussef Canal at Samalut.

Rolling Stock.—There are 20 engines and 200 wagons. A train consists of one brake van and thirteen 5-ton wagons—useful load, 65 tons.

Sand.—Sand gives trouble on this line; it drifts over it very rapidly if there is a strong wind.

This line is still working, but with a greatly reduced traffic.

Item No. 3.—Western Frontier Force

Extension west of Kharga Oasis.—There was a line from the Nile Valley to Kharga Oasis before the war.

Length.—195 kilometres.

Gauge.—2 feet 6 inches.

Gradient.—1 in 30 on worst section, which is that leading down to the Oasis itself.

Materials.—41¼-lb. rails. Steel sleepers mainly, but some wooden.

Rolling Stock.—Four engines, 24 ten-ton wagons. The engines are powerful for this class of line.

Composition of train.—An engine can pull 10 ten-ton wagons up the steepest gradient.

It was decided to extend this line to a point 30 kilometres west of Kharga in order to reach a part of the country which was comparatively free from drift-sand and more suitable for motor-cars.

The line is still working, but with a greatly reduced traffic.

Work on Egyptian State Railways

Traffic.—The work on these lines has been much increased by the army. There are troop and hospital trains to be dealt with, and supplies, stores and ammunition as well. A table is attached which will show the traffic dealt with during 1916.

EGYPTIAN STATE RAILWAYS

SUMMARY OF MILITARY TRANSPORTS DURING 1916

Special Troop Trains Run (including Camel Trains, Specials for Labourers, &c.)

Number of Trains.				Officers.	Other Ranks.	Horses and Mules.	Camels.	Guns and Carts.	Ammunition.	Baggage.
Infantry.	Cavalry.	Special.	Total.						Tons.	Tons.
1,118	577	1,019	2,714	30,346	1,032,659	155,436	56,198	28,043	2,095	47,732

Military Transports by Ordinary Passenger and Goods Trains

Officers.	Other Ranks.	Horses and Mules.	Ammunition.	Supplies and Stores.
			Tons.	Tons.
97,254	983,152	62,431	19,015	1,058,128

Grand Total of Military Transports, Year 1916

Officers.	Other Ranks.	Horses and Mules.	Camels.	Guns and Vehicles.	Ammunition.	Baggage, Stores and Supplies.
					Tons.	Tons.
127,600	2,016,811	217,867	56,198	28,043	21,110	1,105,860

Number of sick, wounded, and convalescents transported in hospital trains, 1916:—
Number of trains, 509; number transported, 77,959.

The State Railways are feeling the loss of rolling stock and engines sent east of the Canal, but not seriously so far. When the force is increased more wagons will be needed on the State lines for collecting and distributing food, etc., for the army, and, with this and the necessity for sending more wagons east of the Canal shortly, there will certainly not be enough rolling stock to meet the usual demands made by the public during the cotton season. Cotton and seed will have to be moved more slowly. This will probably lead to complaints, but is unavoidable.

Workshops.—Besides the extra repairs to rolling stock necessitated by the extra traffic, a great deal of special work has been done in the workshops, such as construction of and repairs to wagons of all sorts, making camel saddles, parts of guns and machine guns, bombs, etc. Extra men have been taken on to deal with this work, or to take the place of men who are employed on it.

APPENDIX F

EGYPTIAN LABOUR CORPS

JANUARY, 1916, TO JUNE, 1917

Organisation, Recruiting and Development

WITH the exception of the Naval wing, which is still at Mudros, the Egyptian Labour Corps, after proving a useful unit during the Gallipoli campaign, returned to Egypt in January, 1916.

Headquarters were at Alexandria, and only 500 men were working at Mersa Matruh.

The Engineer-in-Chief asked for 500 men for work on the Canal, and on the 7th January these arrived, and were distributed equally between Port Said, Ballah, Ismailia, Serapeum and Suez Docks. Shortly after this, camps were opened at Shallufa, El Kubri, Ayun Musa, Ferry Post and Kantara, bringing the strength up to 1,000 men, all for Royal Engineer services.

During February and March, demands for labour were continuously received from A.S.C. and Ordnance, and the numbers employed by the Engineer-in-Chief were increased. Sanitary gangs were asked for by medical services, to undertake the sanitary fatigues in all camps. By the end of April the strength of the corps was 42 officers and 9,000 men.

In order to meet the persistent demands for men, the formation of a recruiting department under the Egyptian Labour Corps was necessary, the establishment being one officer, one doctor and one native clerk for each 10,000 men of the corps.

During May, 5,000 additional men were indented for by the Engineer-in-Chief and obtained with ease; 150 of them were despatched to El Amaid for road-making, and it is interesting to

APPENDIX F

note that the road constructed was first made by the Romans, repaired by Napoleon, and remade by the Egyptian Labour Corps.

Also, during May and June, four new camps were established in Upper Egypt at Kharga, Samalut, Shusha and Fayum. These camps were at first administered separately from Alexandria, but later on an Officer Commanding, Upper Egypt, with headquarters at Minia, became necessary.

During June and July the strength at Kantara and in the Katia area increased considerably to meet military requirements, and it was found necessary for purposes of administration to divide the Canal into three sections.

During June it had been found possible to reduce the pay of unskilled labour to T.P. 5 per day without impairing the efficiency of the corps.

In July a depôt was formed at Hadra Camp for recruiting and training volunteers for Egyptian Labour Corps and other units required. The training of 1,000 drivers for horse transport units was at once put in hand. They were drafted into divisional trains, thus replacing an equivalent number of British troops.

On 2nd August, instructions were received to recruit all the men required by the Camel Transport Corps and to attest them for continuous service at a pay of T.P. 7 per day. This pay was afterwards reduced to T.P. 6, and 19,000 camel-drivers were recruited up to 30th November, and all demands for drivers met in the promptest manner.

Owing to the fact that Egyptian Labour Corps labourers serve on a three months' contract, it is necessary to recruit one-third of the total strength of the corps each month.

As all men under orders for overseas must be trained, a second large depôt was formed on Roda Island, Cairo, for recruiting and training volunteers.

Recruiting.—As the demand for Egyptian Labour Corps men increased, it became necessary to open recruiting camps.

The first camp for recruiting was opened at Assiut, Upper Egypt, on the 16th October, 1916, which was followed by a second camp, with the same object, at Sohag, 90 miles south of Assiut.

Both these camps have proved of great value, and men can

now be collected in the camps and despatched to the coast by special trains in drafts of 2,000.

On 12th February, 1917, a separate recruiting service was formed for recruiting men in Upper Egypt for the Camel Transport Corps, and Middle and Lower Egypt were developed as a recruiting area for the Egyptian Labour Corps.

On 8th May, 1917, recruiting for all services was taken over by a recruiting department, which is now being developed.

The following recruiting figures are of interest :—

Recruited by the Egyptian Labour Corps for Egyptian Labour Corps from 1st January, 1916, to 12th February, 1917	127,862	
Recruited by the Egyptian Labour Corps for Camel Transport Corps during the same period	28,305	
		156,167
Recruited by the Egyptian Labour Corps from 13th February, 1917, to 8th May, 1917, in Lower Egypt for Egyptian Labour Corps		27,599
Recruited by special recruiting service from 13th February, 1917, to 8th May, 1917, for Egyptian Labour Corps		7,235
Recruited by new recruiting department from 9th May, 1917, to 23rd June, 1917, for Egyptian Labour Corps		23,086
		214,087

Egyptian Labour Corps men working in Egypt and Palestine are engaged on a three months' contract.

Egyptian Labour Corps men for overseas are engaged on a six months' contract, dating from the day of embarkation.

In September, 1916, contractors' men were replaced by Egyptian Labour Corps on the east bank of the Canal. The numbers have decreased in the southern section, but have increased considerably in the northern section, *i.e.* on Palestine Lines of Communication and East Force.

The total strength of the corps now is 51,000 labourers, distributed as hereunder :—

	Officers.	Non-commissioned Officers.	Privates.	Other Ranks.
Palestine Lines of Communication and East Force	138	127	255	25,000
Canal Zone and Sundries	62	108	162	5,600
Naval Wing—				
Mudros	2	1	—	903
Suez Docks	2	3	—	380
Port Said	1	3	—	308
Beach (Southern Palestine)	3	3	—	275
Wing "H," Basrah (including those afloat)	18	52	—	7,821
France	48	166	126	9,072
France (awaiting orders)	6	22	10	1,200
Salonica	3	5	—	610

Wing "H," consisting of 2,000 unskilled and 500 skilled labourers (including 13 different trades), sailed for Mesopotamia during September, 1916, and on their arrival an additional 2,000 men were immediately asked for.

During October, November and December, drafts were sent out to Wing "H," until the total number of Egyptian Labour Corps men in Mesopotamia reached 8,000.

Owing to the difficulty of obtaining sufficient officers with a knowledge of Arabic and accustomed to dealing with large numbers of natives, authority was obtained in October to enlist non-commissioned officers to replace civilian overseers who were not under military discipline. Steps were immediately taken to recruit and attest men for this grading, and in all cases they volunteered for the period of the war.

The men were selected from British and Allied subjects, the greatest care being exercised in selecting men with a knowledge of the languages necessary. Altogether some 470 non-commissioned officers have been attested, equipped and drilled in Hadra and Roda depôts, and reports on their work from the various camps to which they have been drafted are, so far, satisfactory.

Owing to the large numbers of native labourers employed in the Canal Zone, it became evident that additional police control would be required. The raising of a police force was entrusted to the Egyptian Labour Corps, and authority was given, on 19th April, 1916, to raise a force of 260 men, with the necessary officers.

The duty of this force was the issue and control of passes to cross the Marine Canal and to guard pontoon bridges. This force has grown considerably, and is now employed for guarding stations and camps on Palestine lines of communication and the villages of Southern Palestine. The present strength of the force is 1,000 men.

It is interesting to note that in Mesopotamia Egyptian Labour Corps men have been selected, trained and formed into a police force for policing Baghdad.

Salonica Draft.—A specially trained company for railway construction was requested for work at Salonica.

Company No. 70 was selected and trained for this work and embarked for Salonica in March last. The company was up to establishment, and favourable reports are being received.

French Draft.—During January, 1917, an application was made for the services of Egyptian Labour Corps for France, and it was decided to send 18 companies, having a strength per company of :—

3 officers, 11 non-commissioned officers, 660 men.

Companies Nos. 71 and 72 embarked on 23rd March, 1917, and arrived safely at Marseilles. Later, Companies Nos. 73 to 84 have embarked, and Nos. 85 and 86 are standing by for orders.

It has been decided that the remaining three companies, viz., 87, 88 and 89, will not leave Egypt owing to the lateness of the season and the difficulty of obtaining transport.

Reports from France are so far satisfactory.

Cadets.—Authority was obtained on 14th February, 1917, to invite applications from suitable non-commissioned officers and men of other units to apply for commissioned rank in the Egyptian Labour Corps. A school for the purpose of teaching selected cadets Arabic was organised; 209 cadets passed through this school, out of which 128 were selected and finally obtained temporary commissions on probation, General List, for duty with the Egyptian Labour Corps.

Maltese Wing.—The Classification Committee, whose object it was to obtain information of British subjects living in

APPENDIX F

Egypt, forwarded large numbers of names for interview, and Egyptian Labour Corps officers interviewed all British and Allied subjects wishing to serve. A large number of men came forward, but they were of little value unless drilled and disciplined.

The Egyptian Labour Corps, "Maltese Wing," was organised with a view of giving discipline to this class of man.

The men were invited to attest for the period of the war as soldiers and under the usual conditions and pay.

Although 1s. a day did not prove attractive, the prospect of obtaining promotion to the non-commissioned-officer foreman rank for service with the Egyptian Labour Corps did appeal to Europeans of Allied nations, and altogether 1,043 men have been attested, trained, and are now serving with the Egyptian Labour Corps in Egypt or overseas.

The privates remaining in the wing are working in exposed positions in Palestine, and are well reported on.

Large numbers of the old Zion Mule Corps attested for service, and are proving useful men.

An interesting feature is that Egyptian Labour Corps labourers who have been working with the corps for various terms during the last two years are now offering their services for the period of the war for this wing, with the knowledge that the work will take them into exposed positions.

Administration

With a unit which has developed from 500 to 51,000, the question of organisation and administration has proved one of considerable anxiety. The corps has been reorganised under the company system, which provides for an establishment, viz. :—

Headquarters, General Headquarters	. . .	Officer commanding, adjutant, officer i/c indents and staff.
Base Office, Alexandria	. .	Officer commanding, officer i/c pay duties, officer i/c records.
Branch Headquarters	. each	10,000 men.
Camp Headquarters	. each	1,200—1,800 men.
Company . .	. each	600 men.
Distribution Camp.		
Recruiting Camps "A" and "B".		

The advantages expected to accrue from this reorganisation are :—(*a*) An authorised establishment. (*b*) Mobility of companies. (*c*) Regimental system of accounts. (*d*) Permanent Reises (headmen), with promotion. This is expected to help recruiting, as men will re-volunteer for their old companies. (*e*) Organised recruiting depôts, which will allow recruiting to be continuous and not spasmodic (on receipt of indents for labour) as previously.

Equipment and Rations

Various scales of equipment and rations were laid down for Egypt in summer and winter, and for the men serving overseas, which were ample and much appreciated by the men.

During summer in Egypt and overseas, the men wear a neat khaki uniform, consisting of shorts and a smock, with " E.L.C." worked in red letters on the chest. A suitable head-dress and boots are supplied when the climate or work necessitates them. During winter an ample supply of underclothing is allowed, and a military overcoat. When men become time-expired, these articles are returned to store, disinfected and re-issued.

Rations have proved ample, but a complete system of canteens became necessary, and these have been established to supply the men with every possible want. Sanction has been obtained for the profits from these canteens to be used as compensation for dependents of men who have lost their lives or have been disabled whilst serving in the corps.

Work Completed

Western Frontier Force.—*Coastal Section.*—At Matruh and Sollum, Egyptian Labour Force personnel have laid a Decauville line, built blockhouses, erected sheds, quarried stone, cut roads and constructed piers, where thousands of tons of stores, equipment, guns and armoured cars were unloaded. On one occasion 900 tons were landed and stacked by 150 men in a day. Captured female camels were broken in and formed into a transport unit, which accompanied the column to Sollum,

APPENDIX F

carrying all the stores necessary for the defence of the advanced base.

The corps also provided stretcher-bearer parties at Matruh in connection with the engagements there.

Samalut—Shusha.—Blockhouse line to Baharia was constructed.

Kharga.—Skilled men have constructed the water dump. After a recent collision, the line was cleared by Egyptian Labour Corps men and communication with Egypt re-established, thus enabling supplies to be brought up in time for the troops in the oasis.

Canal Zone.—With the exception of some private contractors working on roads up till July, generally speaking all the labour for the Army has been supplied by the Egyptian Labour Corps on the east bank of the Canal. Supply and ordnance depôts have been worked by Egyptian Labour Corps men. Sanitation of camps has been done by special gangs under the supervision of Sanitary Section, R.A.M.C., and the great bulk of the work of R.E. services has been performed by the Egyptian Labour Corps. A large proportion of huts, stables, messes and recreation rooms have been constructed by the carpenters. It is interesting to note the number of different trades required to keep an army in motion, viz. :—Carpenters, blacksmiths, tinsmiths, rivetters, platelayers, tent-menders, wheelwrights, masons, quarrymen, stonecutters, plumbers, bakers, engine-drivers, stokers, wood-caulkers, boatmen, pipe-hands, painters. Egypt was able to supply all these trades.

Southern Canal Section (including No. 1 and No. 2 Sections).—Egyptian Labour Corps have completed practically all the inner and second line defences. Men working at Shallufa filled and laid on an average 150 sandbags per man per day. Pipe-lines have been laid at all posts, all roads maintained, and many new ones constructed. A narrow-gauge railway has been constructed between El Shatt, Quarantine and Ayun Musa, and extensions of existing lines at other places. Owing to the advance in Southern Palestine and the clearing of the enemy from the Sinai Province, work in the Southern Canal Section has diminished to a considerable extent.

No. 3 Section or Palestine Lines of Communication and

East Force is an exceedingly large area extending from Kantara to the "front" in Palestine.

During the early summer of 1916 the Egyptian Labour Corps was employed at, and, in fact, made every permanent trench east of, Kantara.

The 12-inch pipe-line was carried out to Romani, and the metre-gauge railway constructed.

Later in the summer the important work of building the Romani Redoubts was undertaken and completed by these men. The men soon understood rivetting and wiring, and, although they were constantly bombed, the work proceeded without delay.

Taking into consideration the climate of Romani in July, it is doubtful if British troops could have done the work as well or in the time required.

The men came under fire freely on 4th August. They were also employed as stretcher-bearers and were well reported on.

It is gratifying to know that these men on returning to their villages re-enlisted after a few days, and, in fact, a large number now look on the construction of defences as their profession.

Laying the pipe-line from Kantara to the defences in Palestine for a distance of 160 miles is perhaps the most important work yet done by the Corps.

The work of laying the pipe-line can be divided as below :—

1. Discharging pipes from steamers and loading them on rail trucks.
2. Discharging pipes from trucks and transporting to the pipe-line, often on the shoulders of men.
3. Cutting a way for pipe-line through sandhills and filling in low levels to carry the pipe.
4. Laying the pipe and connecting it.
5. Covering the completed pipe-line.

The total weight of pipes so handled is approximately 12,000 tons.

The A.S.C. largely employ Egyptian Labour Corps men.

At Kantara Depôt over 2,300 men are continuously employed in discharging steamers brought alongside the depôt, and in loading trains for the advanced depôts and dumps at the front. The work usually goes on day and night, and after three months the men certainly require a rest.

At the advanced depôts and dumps Egyptian Labour Corps men are also working by day and night. The work is well organised. It is interesting to watch a train steam into a depôt, to see the men spring on the trucks, and in the shortest possible time the empty train steams out again.

A service by sea is also maintained to a beach in Southern Palestine, where Egyptian Labour Corps boatmen, stevedores and men discharge stores from transports into surf boats, and from the boats to the beach.

As there is little or no surf boating in Egypt, the work at first was not good; but the men soon learned what was required, and the average weight discharged increased to 31.6 tons per hour over a period; the best day's work being 628 tons with 18 boats.

Defence Work.—After the battle of Romani on 4th August there was a great deal of cleaning up to do, and the defences to repair and complete.

The pipe-line layers were always working in advance of the defence workers, but El Abd, Mazar, El Arish and Rafa were fortified by the Corps, without difficulty or outside help.

At El Arish materials were carried long distances by the men through heavy sand without complaint, and it is generally thought that the men take an interest in their work.

Ordnance Department.—During the latter part of 1916, and to date, the Egyptian Labour Corps has been employed in ordnance depôts, and, as various tradesmen were required, it was necessary to train men specially for this service.

It is anticipated that the men so employed will prove of great value to Egypt after the war.

Ammunition is now discharged and stored in dumps by Egyptian Labour Corps men at a cost of 5d. per ton, average weight per man per day being .3 ton.

Pay and Records.—The development of the Corps from 500 men to over 50,000 in 18 months has put a great strain on the Pay and Record Departments at the Base Office, Alexandria.

Each man when recruited is paid 100 piastres advance, and he probably receives two advances during his period of service and the final payment on discharge. The Records are kept on a modified Army system, but provide sufficient detail to allow of the relatives of any man being communicated with immediately in case of casualties. It is interesting to note that no soldier or Englishman of military age is employed on the clerical staff of the Corps.

Egypt has contributed her man-power towards the prosecution of the war without interference in any way with the cultivation of the country. This has only been possible owing to the fact that the woman- and child-power had been so splendidly developed in pre-war days.

APPENDIX G

CAMEL TRANSPORT CORPS
JANUARY, 1916, TO JUNE, 1917

1. *General Remarks.*—At the end of December, 1915, orders were given for the raising of two Camel Transport Corps, each of 10,000 camels. At this time, there was in existence on the Canal one company of about 800 camels, fully equipped and with its full personnel. This was at once raised to 2,000, the strength fixed for the establishment of the new companies, and the Ministry of Interior commenced the purchase of camels on a large scale. By the end of February, the strength of the companies reached 18,923 camels; this has since been increased, and the present number is about 33,594. Companies were organised and marched out of depôt as follows :—

" A " Company, in existence on Canal Zone.
" B " Company, 13th January, 1916, to Canal Zone.
" C " Company, 17th January, 1916, to Mobile Column, Sollum.
" D " Company, 10th February, 1916, to Canal Zone.
" E " Company, 5th February, 1916, to Canal Zone.
" F " Company, 15th February, 1916, to Canal Zone.
" G " Company, 21st February, 1916, to Canal Zone.
" H " Company, 1st March, 1916, to Western Frontier Force.
" I " Company, 1st March, 1916, formed at Suez.
" K " Company, 1st July, 1916, to Canal Zone.
" L " Company, 11th September, 1916, to Canal Zone.
" M " Company, 26th September, 1916, to Canal Zone.
" N " Company, 14th September, 1916, to Canal Zone.
" O " Company, 6th October, 1916, to Western Frontier Force (in relief of " C " Company, to Canal Zone).

"P" Company, 3rd November, 1916, to Western Frontier Force.
"Q" Company, 4th February, 1917, East Force.
"R" Company, 20th April, 1917, East Force.

These animals were all clipped and dressed for mange three times before being sent out to work.

Since the beginning of the year, "P," "Q" and "R" Companies have been sent to East Force. "H" Company has been brought in from the Western Frontier Force and reorganised at Kantara, the Western Frontier Force being supplied with transport from No. 1 Depôt, in detachments at Baharia 200 camels, Matruh 250 camels, and Sollum 250 camels. "O" Company, which is composed of female camels, has been transferred from the Western Frontier Force to the Canal Zone.

2. *British Personnel.*—Of the officers who joined at the formation of the Corps, one had had six months' experience with the hired transport companies, and one for a month. The first companies that were formed were officered by officials who were lent by the Egyptian Government, and by gentlemen who had been some years in Egypt in business: though they had no military experience or knowledge of camel transport, they had the advantage of knowing the language and the natives. A year's experience has proved that, for the successful working of transport with native drivers, a knowledge of this kind is very necessary. The officer commanding company and adjutant should always have local knowledge. About 50 per cent. of officers were recruited locally.

3. *Native Personnel.*—When the corps was formed, native drivers were recruited from the villages of Upper and Lower Egypt on a three months' contract. Their period of engagement has now been extended to six months, which has greatly improved the efficiency. They have continued to work well, and their conduct has been very satisfactory. The past six months have been very trying, but their behaviour under fire in all cases has been exemplary. Several instances have occurred of natives showing particular devotion to duty, and these have been rewarded under No. G.R.O. 2491, dated 23rd May, 1917. Over 380 have been admitted to hospital from wounds from

APPENDIX G

camel bites, about 70 of whom have lost a limb. At present the total native personnel employed numbers 20,000.

4. *Classes of Camels.*—Eight classes of animals have been received :—

(1) Delta heavy camel.
(2) Upper Egypt camel.
(3) Sudan camel.
(4) Indian Camel Corps.
(5) Somali camel.
(6) Egyptian female camel.
(7) Western desert camel.
(8) Algerian camel.

The best animal up to date has been the heavy Delta baggage camel; the better class of Sudan camel has also done well, but he takes a long time to acclimatise. The Indian camels, though given time to acclimatise, were a failure, and they had a very heavy casualty list, though not hard-worked. The Somali camel soon settles down, but his carrying capacity is small, being limited to 250 lbs. The female camels have done well what little they have had to do, but their value must be put to a longer test. 4,078 Algerian camels have been received as remounts. The majority of these camels are small in size, compared with the heavy-burden Egyptian. They arrived in the country with very heavy, long, hairy coats, and very soft in condition. The majority of them have not yet been put to work, so that it is impossible to say whether they will be a success or not.

The dealing with mange has been a continual trouble, but it has been most successfully treated. The camel is a difficult and delicate animal to work, and casualty lists in all campaigns in which he has been used have been very high. Over 30,000 camels were worked during the first 11 months of last year, and of these 1,473 died, 202 were killed in action, 189 sold owing to injuries, and 7,741 admitted to hospital; and though the number of hospital cases seems large, it should be borne in mind that hardly 50 per cent. of all camels were received with clean backs. There has been a marked decrease in the number of casualties during the last six months, it having been reduced to 2.4 per cent. during the month of May. The casualties of animals killed in action have increased, 188 having been killed during that period. A certain number of casualties occurred at two periods owing to excessive heat.

5. *Equipment.*—Beyond 750 Egyptian Army pack-saddles which were issued to the first company, no saddlery was available from the Ordnance Depôt. Camels began to arrive quickly, and contracts were entered into for the supply of 20,000 saddles, but owing to wood and rope not being available, both contractors failed to supply anything like the required numbers. Camel purchasers were asked to purchase the native saddle with the camels. This was done, and in this way some 10,000 saddles were received, but all had to be overhauled, retied, pads restuffed, girths, breastplates and cruppers renewed and made from any rope that could be procured, and as a rule it took two saddles as received to make one strong enough for military transport work. This overhauling and remaking of saddles was undertaken in workshops at the Camel Depôt and in workshops of departments of the Egyptian Government. The great advantage of these saddles was that they were made of seasoned wood; they were put in serviceable condition at an average cost of P.T. 20 per saddle; all have given 12 months' or more hard work, and a great many are still being used. During the year several types of saddles have been experimented with, and we have as a result two sizes of saddles which are working well. The Indian pattern saddle did excellently for the Indian camel, but, owing to the different shape of the Egyptian camel's back, is unsuitable for that animal. Experiments were also tried with the captured Turkish saddles, with unfavourable results. An improvement has lately been made in girths, to enable them to be tightened at any time when the camel is loaded.

Head-collars.—The Egyptian Army pattern is the only practical one; others were tried, but were not successful. Last winter sacks were used as rugs, but this year a camel-rug made from old blankets and sacks by the Ordnance Department is being used with some success.

6. *Loads.*—The average load carried was 350 lbs. over very heavy desert on the eastern side. The marches in most cases were not long, but, owing to operations, the animals at times remained loaded for long hours. Of good camel grazing there was at first very little, but lately some good grazing has been reached.

INDEX

INDEX

ABASAN EL KEBIR, 142, 154
Abbassia, 123
Abu Aweigila, 98, 99, 100, 101; — Darem, 60; — Hamra, 68, 69, 73; — Hereira, 142, 143, 144, 146, 156, 163, 165
Acknowledgments and Commendations, 38-41, 54, 73-4, 77-82, 108-9, 114, 122-6, 160, 161, 173-8
Adye, Maj.-Gen. J., 41, 125, 177
Aerodromes, 45-6, 95
Aeroplane attacks, 14, 27, 34, 35-6, 45-6, 60, 93, 100, 107, 138, 154, 164, 167; — reconnaissances, 13, 27, 48, 55, 59, 74, 98, 99, 100, 102, 104, 107, 109, 138, 163; — repair, 170; — survey, 9-10
Agostino, Majer da, 172
Ain Sudr, 21, 113
Aircraft and artillery, 109
Akaba, 113
Alexandria, 5, 8, 40, 125
Ali el Muntar, 134, 145, 146, 147, 148, 150, 151, 155, 156, 157, 158, 159, 161, 162
Altham, Gen. Sir Edward, 16, 82, 91
Ammunition raids, 20
Amr, 166
Animal transport services, 174-5
Arab camelry, 57; — snipers, 169
Arabs, agreement with, 170-1
Armoured cars, 20, 114, 117, 118, 119, 120, 121, 122, 123, 139, 140, 150, 170; — trains, 55, 78
Army Brigades:
  2nd Dismounted, 19
  5th Mounted, 23, 51, 63, 64, 66, 67, 73, 90, 105, 106, 144; 6th, 160; 22nd, 146, 148
  125th, 64; 127th, 55, 64, 67; 156th, 67, 72, 159, 161; 159th, 144, 145, 159; 160th, 63, 144, 145, 150; 161st, 145, 147, 150, 153, 160; 162nd, 159, 160, 162; 163rd, 159, 160; 229th of 74th Div., 162
  155th Infantry, 65, 159, 160, 161, 162; 158th, 65, 74, 144, 145
Army Corps:
  8th, 13; 9th, 11, 13; 15th, 11, 13, 14, 23
Army Divisions:
  11th, 13; 13th, 13; 42nd, 59, 62, 63, 64, 65, 66, 67, 68, 73, 90, 91, 92, 99, 110, 130, 131; 46th, 135; 52nd, 23, 56, 67, 68, 69, 72, 73, 90, 91, 93, 99, 136, 140, 141, 142, 149, 153, 155, 157, 158, 161, 162, 173; 53rd, 11, 16, 36-7, 55, 91, 92, 93, 109, 110, 130, 139, 142, 144, 145, 147, 148, 149, 150, 151, 153, 156, 157, 158, 162, 173; 54th, 11, 16, 62, 109, 110, 130, 140, 141, 142, 144, 148, 149, 150, 151, 152, 153, 155, 157, 158, 161, 162, 173; 74th, 132, 136-7, 140, 156, 158, 162; 75th, 137, 166
Army Postal Service, 81
Asluj, 168, 169
Assiut, 19
Assuan, 17, 18, 117
Atawineh ridge, 155, 156, 158
Aulad Ali tribes, 38
Australian and New Zealand Army Corps, 4, 5, 7, 11, 21, 36, 46, 47, 49, 135, 136; — — Mounted Division, 7, 21, 24, 34, 35, 47, 51, 54, 56, 59, 63, 67, 68, 73, 75, 90, 91, 92, 93, 98, 99, 101, 105, 135, 143, 144, 146, 147, 148, 157, 158, 164, 168, 169, 173
Australian Light Horse, 36, 46, 75, 89; — —, 1st Regt., 47, 64, 69, 71, 99, 102, 103, 105, 106; 2nd, 24, 35, 64, 69, 71, 101, 143, 146, 148; 3rd, 59, 63, 65, 66, 68, 99, 101, 103, 105, 106, 107, 146, 147, 150, 160; 4th, 78, 159, 160; 5th, 27; 9th, 21-2; 10th, 103; 11th, 61, 69, 113
Austrian Hospital, 40
Austrians, 57, 134
Ayrshire Battery, R.H.A., 36, 73, 75

Baiket el Sana, 158
Bailloud, M. le Général, 172
Bardia, 37, 48
Barrani, 37, 38
Bawitti, 115
Bedfordshire Regt., 1/5th, 76
Bedouins, 37-8, 48, 55, 111, 112, 113
Beersheba, 93, 100, 109, 133, 135, 138, 139, 140, 142, 167
Beit Durdis, 143
Beris, 38, 117
Bikanir Camel Corps, 21, 22, 46, 48, 73-4, 79, 135, 136, 137, 140, 170, 173

223

Bir Abu el Afein, 35, 58; — Abu Tif, 113; — el Abd, 22, 23, 24, 27, 34, 35, 47, 55, 56, 57, 58, 70, 71, 72, 73, 90, 92, 94, 96, 97; — el Aweidiya, 65, 70; — el Bayud, 25, 27, 47, 55, 56, 60, 71, 72, 90; — el Dueidar, 24, 26, 27, 28, 35, 53, 55, 62, 63, 65, 66, 68; — el Esani, 167, 168; — el Giddi, 22; — el Hamisah, 24, 25, 26, 63, 68; — el Hassana, 13, 14, 90, 99, 108, 112; — el Jameil, 55, 56; — el Jefeir, 47, 69; — el Jifjaffa, 21-2; — el Mageibra, 23, 25, 47, 56, 57, 58, 60, 65, 69, 70, 72; — el Maghara, 89, 90, 99, 108; — el Masmi, 92, 93, 99; — el Mazar, 36, 55, 72, 75, 76, 90, 92, 93, 94, 99, 110; — el Nuss, 14, 63, 68; — el Tawal, 76; — el Themada, 113; — Etmaler, 62, 67; — Lahfan, 93, 112; — Mabeiuk, 21, 100; — Rodh Salem, 36; — Saba, 169; — Salmana, 36, 54, 90; — Sheikh Mohammed, 115; — um Gurf, 92
Blackburn, Major H., R.F.C., 74
Blair, Brig.-Gen. E. McL., R.E., 54
Blockhouses, 37
Borton Pasha, N.T., 81
Bowman-Manifold, Brig.-Gen., 39-40
British West Indies Regt., 174
Budkhulu, 115
Byng, Lt.-Gen. Sir Julian, 11, 13

Caccia, Capt., 121
Cactus hedges, 148, 156
Cairo, 4, 16, 79, 91, 93, 176
Camel Maxim Section, 79; — patrolling, 38, 70; — transport, 12, 15, 59, 95, 100, 111, 151; — Transport Corps, 6, 7, 19, 49, 123, 136, 174 (see Appendix G)
Camels, 12, 20, 35, 36, 52, 54, 59, 72, 76, 77, 79, 95, 96, 139, 217-20
Campbell, Maj.-Gen. Sir Walter, 41, 125, 177
Camps, desert, 94-5
Canal Defences, 10-12, 13, 14-15, 33, 39, 40, 47, 50, 58, 79, 91, 109; — Section, Northern, 50, 51, 53, 61, 91, 110, 171; ——, Southern, 50, 51, 91, 100, 109, 110, 113, 171
Canterbury (N.Z.) Mounted Rifles, 35, 60
Captures, 20, 22, 35, 36, 48, 49, 56, 67, 68, 70, 72, 75-6, 76, 77, 103, 104, 105-6, 106-7, 112, 113, 114, 115, 116, 121, 143, 153, 169, 172
Casson, Brig.-Gen. H. G., 140
Casualties, 21, 22, 25, 26, 27, 34, 36, 46, 66, 70, 71, 75, 77, 78, 93, 104, 108, 121, 153, 160, 163, 169
Chaplains' Dept., 175
Chauvel, Maj.-Gen. H. G., 21, 56, 68, 73, 101, 102, 103, 105, 108, 109, 146, 147, 149, 164
Chaytor, Brig.-Gen. E. W. C., 101, 102, 164
Cheshire Field Company, 19; — Yeomanry, 69-70
Chetwode, Lt.-Gen. Sir Philip, Bt., 94, 104, 106, 107, 108, 109, 138, 164, 165, 177
Church Army, 175
Clothing, 80
Coastal Section, 18, 111, 171
Colston, the Hon. E. M., 8
Communications, officers of, 5, 54, 91, 172-3
Como, Capt., Italian Navy, 48
Conditions peculiar to Egypt, 8, 37
Conquering the desert, 94-5
Coventry, Lt.-Col., 25, 26
Cox, Maj.-Gen. Sir H. V., 7, 21
Crops destroyed, 169-70
Cyprus, 32, 33

Dallas, Maj.-Gen. A. G., 38, 46, 74, 144
Darb el Rubi, 37
Dardanelles Army, 3, 5, 79, 173
Darut es Sharif, 17
Davies, Brig.-Gen. G. F., 174
Davies, Lt.-Gen. Sir Francis, 13
Daylight, 149
Deir el Belah, 141, 152, 153, 154, 155, 166, 167
De Knoop, Major J. J., 69, 70
Delta District Command, 16, 140
Demolitions, 20, 22, 25, 35, 36, 47, 73, 76, 100, 168, 169, 170, 172
Denbighshire Yeomanry, 19
Desert advance, work of, 94-5; — Column, 91, 92, 94, 95-6, 99, 104, 108, 110, 137, 139, 140, 141, 142, 146, 149, 156, 157, 158, 160, 163, 164, 166, 169, 170; — water problem, 96, 97-8, 103, 149
Dhabba, 18, 38, 118
Dobell, Maj.-Gen. Sir Charles, 48, 76, 91, 101, 104, 108, 112, 137, 149, 163, 164, 165
Douglas, Maj.-Gen. Sir W., 47, 73
Dowson, Mr. E. M., 9
Dual control, 16
Durbars, 115, 116

Eastern Force, 91, 91-2, 137, 138, 139, 141, 142-3, 149, 150, 151, 152, 153,

INDEX 225

155, 162, 163, 164, 165, 171; — Front, 14, 46, 50, 51, 54, 89, 90
Egypt, concentration in, 3, 5; defence of, 4; command in, unified, 15–16; freed from formed bodies of the enemy, 125; collecting troops in, 140; restrictions on leaving or entering, 171
Egyptian Army, 14, 78–80; — — Cavalry, 19, 79; — — Hospital, 79; — — Stores Dept., 80
Egyptian Expeditionary Force, 17, 49–50, 78, 79, 80, 135–7, 176 (see Appendix C); — Government, 39; — Labour Corps, 54, 95, 123–4, 136, 174 (see Appendix F); — Military Works Dept., 79; — Postal Service, 81
El Ageila, 116; — Amaid, 19, 20; — Arish, 12, 13, 35, 36, 45–6, 50, 58, 72, 75, 76, 90, 91, 92, 93, 94, 97, 98, 99, 100, 101, 103, 104, 109, 110, 111, 112, 122, 129, 130, 131, 132, 137, 140, 142, 171, 172; — Auja, 100, 167, 168, 169, 172; — Burjaliya ridge, 150; — Ferdan, 55, 92; — Hammame, 18, 38; — Kubri, 76, 77; — Magdhaba, 93, 98, 99, 100, 101, 102, 103, 104, 108; — Magruntein, 104, 108, 109, 110; — Mendur, 143; — Rabah, 26, 63, 69, 72; — Sheluf, 144, 145; — Sire ridge, 150, 155; — Tine, 165, 167
Embarkations from Egypt, Jan. 9 to May 31, 1916, 180–3
Enemy air-raids, 28, 34, 92–3, 109, 153–4, 167, 172; — forces, 10, 17, 26, 33, 56–7, 58, 98, 134, 150, 151, 155, 165; — plans, 12, 13, 15; — raids, 23, 25–6; — supplies, measures against, 18, 20, 21, 46
Engineer services, 175

Fayum, 18, 116
Feint to detain Turks, 32–3
Filter-plant, 52, 53, 94
Flying Column, 101; takes El Magdhaba, 101–4
Food, 20, 38, 95, 171
Ford cars, 118, 121
Forrest, Major W. T., 160
France, 7, 14, 36, 46, 49, 131, 136
French troops, 172

Gaafer captured, 16
Gallipoli campaign, 4; troops, 5; survey experience, 9; hospital cases, 80, 81

P

Garrison Battalions, 33, 50, 135, 140, 174
Garrisons, 10, 13, 14, 25, 26, 33, 65, 78, 79, 115, 170
Gaza, 129, 132, 133, 134, 135, 138, 140, 141, 142, 143, 144, 145, 146, 147, 148, 149, 150, 152, 153, 154, 155, 156, 157, 158, 159, 163, 165, 167, 168, 173
Gebel Lamlaz, 118
General Headquarters, Cairo, 4, 91; Ismailia, 11, 16; El Arish, 142; Khan Yunus, 155, 164
German equipment, 57
Germans, 57, 106, 107–8, 134, 153, 156
Gilban, 53, 63
Girdwood, Maj.-Gen. E. S. B., 140
Gloucestershire Hussars, 22, 144; — Yeomanry, 24, 25, 26, 66
Godley, Lt.-Gen. Sir A. J., 11, 21, 37
Gordon, Maj.-Gen. the Hon. F., 32
Grant, Lt.-Col., 70
Gray, Brig.-Gen. F. W. B., 33
Great Bitter Lake, 113
Green Hill, 156, 161

Hare, Maj.-Gen. S. W., 145, 161
Harra Wells, 114–15
Health, 38, 164, 166, 174
Hedjaz, 58, 172
Helles, Cape, 3
Herbert, Brig.-Gen. E. A., 77
Hertfordshire Yeomanry, 76
Hod Abu Dhababis, 47; — Amoia, 60; — el Aras, 65, 66; — el Bada, 65; — el Bayud, 35, 47, 70; — el Dhakar, 69; — el Enna, 64, 65, 68; — el Gadadia, 36; — el Ge'eila, 47; — el Masia, 58, 70; — el Muhammat, 70; — el Mushalfat, 47, 71; — el Negiliat, 58, 69; — el Reshafat, 34, 69; — el Sagia, 35, 69; — Salmana, 35, 72; — um el Dhaunnin, 47; — um Ugba, 14, 60
Hodgson, Maj.-Gen. H. W., 118, 119, 121, 139
Homossia, 72
Hong Kong and Singapore Mountain Battery, 19, 75, 102, 105, 123, 140
Hon. Artillery Company, 106
Hordern, Brig.-Gen. A. V. C., 175
Horne, Lt.-Gen. Sir H. S., 11, 23
Horse-artillery, 102
Horses, 72, 96, 103, 139, 149, 152
Hospitals, 40, 80, 81, 104
Huj, 142, 143, 144, 150

Imbros, 3, 11, 33
Imperial Camel Corps, 6, 7, 19, 38, 48, 49, 60–1, 75, 77, 115, 117, 123, 136,

137, 152, 172, 173; Imperial Camel Corps Brigade, 98, 99, 101, 102, 103, 105, 106, 107, 139–40, 141, 142, 143, 146, 148, 149, 150, 151, 156, 157, 158, 159, 160, 168, 169, 170
Imperial Mounted Division, 139, 143, 144, 146, 147, 148, 158; — Service Cavalry Brigade, 135, 136, 173
Indian Camel Corps, 7; — Infantry, 50, 113, 135, 136, 137, 173
In Seirat, 141, 142, 143, 154, 156
Intelligence Branch, 9
Inverness Battery, R.H.A., 73, 75
Ismailia, 7, 10, 11, 16, 91, 92
Italian Commanders, 37, 48; — co-operation, 48–9; — Government, 37; — troops, 37, 172

Jaghbub, 117, 118, 121
Jerusalem, 133, 134, 138, 153
Joubert, Lt.-Col. P. B., R.F.C., 74

Kantara, 12, 15, 27, 52, 53, 55, 62, 74, 90, 94
Kasr, 115
Katia, 9, 12, 14, 15, 22, 23, 24, 25, 26, 27, 28, 34, 35, 55, 56, 58, 63, 64, 68, 69, 72, 96
Katib Gannit Hill, 62, 63, 64
Khalasa, 168
Khan Yunus, 93, 105, 112, 138, 141, 142, 144, 153, 155, 156, 172
Khirbet Sihan, 159, 160
King's Messengers, 124
Kitchener, Lord, 51
Kressenstein, Col. Kress von, 57
Kurd Hill, 155, 157

Labyrinth, 147, 156
Lawrence, Maj.-Gen. the Hon. H. A., 23, 34, 47, 62, 63, 64, 65, 66, 73
Lees Hill, 156, 159
Legalit Gate, 115, 116
Leicester Battery, R.H.A., 73
Lemnos, 11, 33
Levant, 5 (note), 16
Liddell, Lt.-Col. J. S., R.E., 40
Light car patrols, 20, 48, 116, 117, 118, 120, 122, 123, 140, 150, 170
Lines of Communication Defences, 16, 77, 125, 171–2, 172–3
Lloyd, Lt.-Col. A. H. O., 19
London, City of, Yeomanry, 61, 69; — Regiment, 1/10th, 76
Lubbock, Lt.-Col. G., R.E., 54
Lynden-Bell, Maj.-Gen. Sir Arthur, 40, 81, 125, 177

Macauley, Col. Sir George, R.E., 39, 54, 122
Macdonald, Col. Sir Murdoch, 39
MacGay, Maj.-Gen. the Hon. J., 21
McMahon, Lt.-Col. Sir A. H., High Commissioner, 39
McNeill, Lt.-Col. A., 19
Mahemdia, 34, 35, 47, 60, 62, 63, 65, 72
Maher, Surgeon-Gen. J., 174
Mahon, Lt.-Gen. Sir B. T., 28, 32, 38
Maintenance of Forces, 5, 6
Mangles, Capt. C. G., 48
Mansura Ridge, 144, 145, 150, 151, 154, 155, 157, 162
Maps, 9
Marriott-Dodington, Brig.-Gen. W., 147
Masaid, 90, 92, 93, 97, 98, 99, 111
Maxwell, Gen. Sir John, 4, 11, 14, 15, 16, 17
Medical Corps, 174
Mediterranean Expeditionary Force, 3, 9, 78, 79, 80 (see Appendix B)
Mejdel, 167
Mendisha, 115
Meredith, Mount, 64
Mersa Matruh, 18, 38, 117, 118, 120, 121
Mesopotamia, 133
Methuen, F.M. the Rt. Hon. Lord, 80
Middlesex Hill, 156, 161; — Regiment, 2/7th, 20; — Yeomanry, 46, 76
Milne, Lt.-Gen. G. F., 32
Mine-sweeping, 99–100
Minya, 19, 20
Mirage delays artillery, 102
Misurata, 48, 49
Mitchell, Capt. F. H., R.N., 17
Moascar, 55, 110
Mobile Column, 61, 65, 69, 70, 71, 74; — defence, 15, 50, 61; — striking force, 96
Mohammed Saleh, 117, 119, 121
Mohariq sand dunes, 37
Monitors, 60, 66, 74, 157, 158
Monro, Gen. Sir G. C., 3
Moraisa, 20, 37
Motor-car raids and reconnaissances, 20, 48–9, 77, 115, 116, 117, 118–21, 122
Motor transport, 118
Mott, Maj.-Gen. S. F., 156
Mudge, Brig.-Gen. A., 76
Mudros, 3, 80
Muhafzia, 20, 48, 49, 117
Murray, Sir Archibald: Takes over command at Cairo, 3; his instruc-

INDEX

tions, 4; organises Canal Defences, 10–12; modifies original scheme, 15, 50–1; appointed to Chief Command, 15–16; determines policy against the Senoussi, 17–19; plans defences of Katia District, 34–5; prepares desert campaign, 51–3; reinforces Eastern Front, 55–6; prepares to attack Turks, 58–9; anticipates enemy's plans, 63; redistributes troops in Eastern Force, 91–2; prepares position covering Bir el Abd, 92; organises advance against El Arish—water supply the decisive factor, 94–8; Turks having abandoned El Arish, arranges pursuit, 100–1; after taking Magdhaba, decides to attack Magruntein, 104; establishes depôt at El Arish, 110–11; takes posts at Hassana and Nekhl, 112–14; occupies Baharia and Dakhla oases, 114–16; sends armoured cars against Siwa and Girba oases and frees Western Front from Senoussi menace, 117–22; recites changes in War Cabinet policy in Egypt, 129–35; discusses strength of Egyptian Expeditionary Force, 135–7; his advance to Gaza and first battle, 137–53; plans and dispositions for second battle, 153–6; advance and second battle of Gaza described, 156–63; decision to break off battle, consolidate ground won and await opportunity for further attack, 163–5

Naval co-operation, 35, 39, 60, 66, 99, 111, 157, 158; — Air Service, 177; — patrol, 17, 18; — reconnaissance, 116–17
Needham, Major H., 33
Negiliat, 90
Nejed, 142
Nekhl, 13, 14, 90, 99, 100, 108, 111, 113
New Zealand Division, 7, 79; — Mounted Rifles Brigade, 36, 63, 65, 66, 67, 99, 101, 102, 103, 105, 106, 107, 112, 146, 147, 148
Nile district, 4, 16, 17, 18, 19, 20, 37, 38, 77–8
Northamptonshire Regt., 1/4th, 76
North Midland Mounted Brigade, 16
Notre Dame de la Délivrance, 40
Nuri, 16, 37, 117
Nursing Services, 40, 81

Oases: Baharia, 18, 19, 37, 38, 48, 77, 114, 115, 116; Dakhla, 18, 19, 38, 48, 114, 115, 116; El Qara, 117; Farafra, 18, 38, 116; Girba, 19, 117, 118, 119, 121; Kharga, 18, 19, 38, 77, 115, 117; Kurkur, 117; Melfa, 171; Moghara, 18, 38, 117; Siwa, 18, 38, 114, 117, 118, 119, 120, 121, 170, 171
Offensive defence, 10, 12
Oghratina, 24, 25, 27, 55, 56, 57, 58, 70
Operations against Turks, 64–74, 98–109, 112–14, 137–53, 153–65; — against Senoussi, 114–16
Ordnance Department, 6
Ottley, Major W. J., 48
Outpost Hill, 156, 159, 160, 161, 162

Palestine advance, 130–2, 133, 134–5, 139; — Lines of Communication Defences, 171–2, 173
Palin, Brig.-Gen. P. C., 92, 114
Passes: Garet el Munasib, 118, 119, 120, 121; Mitla, 100; Neqb el Shegga, 118; Wadi Abu Garawid, 113; — el Baha, 113
Patrol work, 20, 21, 22, 23, 36, 38, 55, 56, 57–8, 75, 77, 78, 92, 93, 94, 98, 107, 111, 115, 116, 117, 167
Ped-rails, 96
Pelusium, 62, 64, 65, 66, 67
Picot, M., 172
Piépape, M. le Col., 172
Piping, 13, 52, 54, 94, 95, 96, 97, 135, 172
Pollen, Lt.-Col. S. H., 125–6, 177–8
Port Said, 5, 10, 11, 91, 100
Port services, 175–6
Prince of Wales, 17
Prisoners, British, 16; enemy, 56–7

Rafa, 99, 104, 105, 107, 108, 109, 111, 130, 132, 135, 140, 141, 166, 168, 172
Railway construction, 12, 13, 18, 23, 28, 31, 48, 49, 52, 53–4, 77, 90, 92, 93, 94, 95, 104, 110, 111, 115, 122, 133, 135, 138, 140, 166 (see Appendix E); — demolition, 168, 169; — transport, 5–6, 19, 39, 53, 97, 110–11
Railways: Baharia, 115; Central Palestine, 138, 139, 165; desert, 95, 96–7; Egyptian State, 6; Mariut, 20; military, 172 (see Appendix E)
Ramle, 138, 167
Ras Abu Zeneima, 14, 48, 79
Reconnaissances, 14, 20, 21, 34, 35, 47, 48, 54, 55, 59, 74, 75, 76–7, 89–90, 92–3, 112, 157, 166
Red Cross, 40, 124
Re-equipment, 5, 6

Reinforcements, British and Australian, 5, 6–7; refused by War Cabinet, 131, 133; arrive from Colonies, 166; promised from Salonica, 166–7; French and Italian, 172
Remount Department, 6, 174
Reorganisation, 5, 6
"Requin," 157, 158
Reservoirs, 52, 53, 94, 95
Roads and road-making, 11, 13, 30–1, 39, 52, 77, 94, 95, 206–7, 212, 213
Roberts, Capt., 26–7
Robinson, Commdr. E., R.N., 74
Rock cisterns, 21, 46, 110
Romani, 24, 25, 26, 28, 34, 35, 53, 55, 56, 62, 63, 64, 65, 72, 90, 91, 93, 94, 95, 96, 97, 109; — battle, 64–74
Royal Australian Naval Bridging Train, 100; — Engineers, 19, 53, 54, 175; — Field Artillery, 51; — Flying Corps, 9, 13, 14, 19, 25, 27, 28, 34, 35, 36, 55, 56, 59, 60, 66, 69, 74, 75, 93, 98, 100, 104, 107, 108–9, 138, 154, 167, 173; — Horse Artillery, 73; — Naval Air Service, 13, 35, 75; — — Division, 33, 39; — Scots Fusiliers, 26, 27; — Welsh Fusiliers, 67
Royston, Brig.-Gen. J. R., 147
Royston, Mount, 65, 66, 67
Russians, 13, 134
Ryrie, Brig.-Gen. G. de L., 148

St. John, Lt.-Commdr. A. O., R.N., 74
St. John of Jerusalem, 40, 124
Salihiya, 24
Salonica, British force at, 4, 5, 32, 49; machine-gun school, 8; General Sarrail in command, 11, 28, 29; defences at, 28; operations, 12 Jan.–30 April, 1916, 28–31; training, 31–2; command changes, 32; enemy movements, 32; hospital cases, 80, 81; reinforcements from, 135, 137; staff course for force, 176
Samalut, 37, 77
Sampson Ridge, 158, 162
Sanitation, 95, 206, 213
Sayed Ahmed, the Grand Senoussi, 114, 117, 118, 119, 121; — Mohammed Idris, 117, 170, 171
School of Instruction, Imperial, 7–8, 16, 176
Schools, machine-gun, 7, 8; staff, 176
Scott, Major, 22
Senoussi defeated, 16; policy against, 17–19, 114; convoy arrested, 77; Egyptian aid against, 79; cleared from oases, 114–16; attacked by armoured cars and cleared from Western Front, 117–22; restrictions against, 171; "zawias," 171
Serapeum, 112
Serionne, Charles, Comte de, 40
Sharqia province, 91
Sharta, 165, 166
Sheikh Abbas, 142, 145, 148, 150, 151, 154, 155, 157, 162–3, 165; — Ahmed, 144; — Ajlin, 158, 162, 165, 167; Zowaid, 93, 99, 111, 138, 139, 140, 141
Shellal, 107, 109, 156, 165, 166
Shropshire Yeomanry, 19
Shusha, 114
Sidi Bishra, 55
Signal services, 8, 39–40, 175; — stations, desert, 95
Sihan, 157
Sikh Pioneers, 23rd, 48
Sikhs, 14th, 14
Sinai, 9, 10, 33, 108, 173; —, coast of, 14; —, desert of, 51, 94
Sirdar, 17, 54
Smith, Lt.-Col. C. L., 60, 65, 70, 74
Smith, Maj.-Gen. W. E. B., 47, 155–6
Sollum, 16, 18, 20, 37, 38, 48, 170, 171
Somerset Battery, R.H.A., 73, 148
South African Infantry Brigade, 135
Staff work, 4, 5, 81–2, 101, 125
Stokes gun batteries, 7, 55
Stone, 94, 212
Sudan, 51, 79; — Administration, 78, 80
Sudr el Heitan, 21, 100
Suez, 10, 11, 91, 93, 112, 113; — Canal, 4, 79, 132, 172; — — Company, 40
Sultan, His Highness the, 38–9, 176
Supply and Transport Dept., 6; — depôt at El Arish, 110–11
Survey work, 8–10
Suvla Bay, 4, 153
Sykes, Col. Sir Mark, Bt., 172
Syria, 10, 13, 32, 58

Tanks, 154, 157, 159
Tel el Jemmi, 154, 167; — el Kebir, 7; — el Sharia, 100, 138, 139, 140, 142, 144, 146, 156, 167
Telegraph Company, Eastern, 40; — — of Egypt, 40
Telegraphs and telegraphists, 8
Tenedos, 11, 33
Tenida, 115
Territorials, 11, 50, 135
Tescione, Lieut., 117
Thompson, Major, 27
Thomson, Sir Courtauld, 40, 124

INDEX

Todd, Lt.-Col. T. J., 46
Topographical Section, 9
Tor, 14, 79
Training, 31-2, 111; — centres, 7
Trench warfare, 164, 170
Troops required, 130, 132, 134
Tugs and steel plates, 80
Turks carry Oghratina and Katia, 25-6; repulsed at Dueidar and pursued, 27, 28; concentrate in Sinai, 33; advance from El Arish, 55, entrench at Oghratina, 56, 57, and still advance, 59-60, 63; force back outpost line along Wellington Ridge, 64-5; foiled by Mahemdia-Romani defences, 65-6; rapid advance of, affects British plan, 66; reach farthest point, 66-7; driven from Mt. Royston and Wellington Ridge with loss, 67, 68; retire from Katia, 69; abandon Oghratina and make last stand near Bir el Abd, 70-1; retire to El Arish, 71-2; losses of, 72-3; on being raided retire from Bir el Mazar, 75-6; surprised at Bir el Tawal, 76-7; aircraft activity of, 92-3; control water-supply at El Arish, 97-8; retire from El Arish and Masud, 98-9; lose Magdhaba, 101-4; entrench at El Magruntein, 104, 105; lose Rafa and El Magruntein and withdraw from Sinai province, 105-9; concentrate near Shellal, 109; lose posts at Khan Yunus, Bir el Hassana and Nekhl, 112-14; question of attacking in Palestine, 130-2; evacuate Weli Sheikh Nuran, 132, 138; strength of, in Palestine, 133, 134; hold Gaza in first battle, 142-53; strengthen defences of Gaza, 155, 156; hold Gaza in second battle, 156-62; begin building railway, 165

Ujret el Zol, 90, 92, 110
Um Aisha, 58; — Jerrar, 154; — Ugba, 26, 34, 35

Wadi el Arish, 97, 101, 102, 103; — el Hesi, 142; — Ginneh, 14; Ghuzze, 133, 135, 140, 141, 142, 143, 144, 145, 149, 152, 154, 155, 156, 157, 165, 166; — Halfa, 17; — Imleih, 157; — Natron, 18, 38, 77; Sanal, 48; — Theigat el Amirin, 169; — um Hamatha, 21; — um Muksheib, 21, 46, 110
War Cabinet policy, v-vi, 129, 130, 131, 133, 134, 153, 165
Warren, the, 156
Warwickshire Yeomanry, 24, 25, 26
Water, saline, 52, 96; — supply, 11, 15, 20, 24, 39, 49, 51, 52-3, 96-8, 103, 110, 133, 149, 152, 154, 172 (see Appendix D)
Watson, Maj.-Gen. W. A., 77-8, 114, 115, 116
Weli Sheikh Nuran, 109, 129, 132, 138, 166
Wellington Ridge, 64, 66, 67, 68, 73
Wemyss, Vice-Admiral Sir Rosslyn, 39, 111, 176-7
Western Desert, 17, 116, 122; — Frontier Force, 16-17, 19, 38, 48, 77, 114, 116, 122, 140
Wharf and pier construction, 52-3, 100
Wiggin, Brig.-Gen., 23, 24, 25, 26
Williams, Maj.-Gen. G., 54
Williamson, Capt. A. H., 100
Wingate, High Commissioner-General Sir F. R., 78, 124, 176
Wireless installations, desert, 95
Worcestershire Yeomanry, 23, 24, 25, 26
Works Department, 6, 175
Wright, Maj.-Gen. H. B. H., 54

Yeomanry, 50, 61, 89, 107, 132, 135, 136, 140, 173
Y.M.C.A., 175
Yorke, Lt.-Col., 22, 26

Zeitoun, 7, 8, 16, 176
Zowia Jansur, 117

www.ingramcontent.com/pod-product-compliance
Lightning Source LLC
Chambersburg PA
CBHW070936180426
43192CB00039B/2246